tu:~# name=HowLinux
name = HowLinux
nd 'name' no found, did yo
command 'mame' from snap man
command 'nvme' from deb n
command 'namei' from deb u
command 'nam' from deb nam
command 'name' from de
command 'named' from de
command 'lame' from de
command 'uname' from de
command 'nama' from de
See 'snap info <snapname>' fo
root@ubuntu:~#

NOAH HERRMANN

# LINUX
## FOR BEGINNERS

How to Master the Linux Operating System and
Command Line from Scratch

# TABLE OF CONTENTS

## Chapter 7: **Alternatives to Windows Applications** ............................ 103



## **Conclusion** ............................................................ 112

# INTRODUCTION

Linux is a free and open-source operating system based on the UNIX and PSOIX programming languages. It is free to download and use. It was built on the Intel x86 paradigm. In reality, compared to the rest of the operating systems, Linux has the most extensive user base.

This is why a Linux-based computer or system is fast and is often even compared to those incredible supercomputers. Unlike other operating systems, Linux can be customized to any form of the system used, while other operating systems are designed for a particular computer type.

This is due to the open-source software collaboration, capable of supporting different libraries and directories.

The next step is to learn more about writing and editing shell scripts and developing automation scripts that will help you get more out of Linux.

The Linux operating system (OS) is not well recognized by the average user, even though it is the most commonly used platform, with applications for Android phones, smartwatches, refrigerators, washing machines, video game consoles, and DVRs.

When you remember how Linux came to be and how it continues to grow, it is awe-inspiring. Linux has evolved from its humble beginnings as a hobby for one human, Linus Torvalds of Finland, to a full-fledged operating system with features that rival any commercial Unix operating system.

To top it off, Linux — along with all of its source code — is free. All you have to do is download it from the Internet or purchase it on CDs or DVDs from one of the many Linux CD sellers for a small fee.

The adage "you get what you pay for" does not apply to Linux. Linux is not a slouch for performance, functionality, and reliability, even though it is free. The way Linux is designed and modified has a lot to do with its robustness. Developers from all over the world work together to add new functionality. Users update incremental versions daily and test them in several device configurations.

Linux revisions are subjected to much more extensive beta testing than consumer applications.

The number of Linux users has increased exponentially since Linux kernel 1.0 on March 14, 1994. Many Linux distributions make installation and usage of the operating system, software, and installation tools easier. Some Linux distributions are sold and subsidized commercially, while others are still freely available.

Unlike many other free downloadable software programs, Linux comes with a wealth of online documentation on topics like downloading and configuring the operating system on several PCs and peripherals. A few hard-core Linux users are proficient enough to use Linux effectively solely based on online documentation. However, a much more significant percentage of users switch to Linux for a particular purpose (such as setting up a web server or learning Linux). Many Linux users still use their machines at home. The online documentation is difficult to use for these new users, as it frequently does not cover the unique uses of Linux that each user might have in mind.

If you are new to Linux, you will need a step-by-step guide that not only guides you through installation and configuration but also explains how to use Linux for a particular mission. Before deciding on a Linux distribution, try out a few.

This book has been written keeping an average person with little to no knowledge in mind. It has been formulated in simple and easy-to-understand language, which makes it equally useful for newbies and professionals.

# CHAPTER 1
# WHAT IS LINUX ABOUT?

Linux began as a pc operating system, but it has since expanded to include servers, supercomputers, data centers, and other devices. Linux is now used in integrated devices such as routers, security controls, TV sets, digital cameras, game consoles, and smartwatches. Android, which is built on the Linux kernel and runs on tablets and smartphones, is Linux's greatest victory. Linux has the highest user base of any particular operating system, thanks to Android. A Linux distribution is a set of Linux packages.

Linux distribution is also an operating system comprised of a range of algorithms centered on the Linux framework or kernel, which includes the Linux kernel and supporting modules and software. You can also get a Linux-based OS by installing one of the Linux distributions, which are available for various devices such as embedded systems, computers, and so on.

## 1.1 What Is an Operating System?

The OS (Operating System) on your computer is in charge of the computer's hardware and software. Several computer applications are usually running simultaneously, and they all need access to your computer's central processing unit (CPU), storage, and memory. This is coordinated by the OS (Operating System) to ensure that each software receives the resources it requires.

Computer software and system development benefit significantly from an OS (Operating System). Without an OS (Operating System), each application must include its user interface and the extensive code required to manage the computer's low-level functions, such as disc storage, network connectivity, and so on. Given the wide range of hardware resources available, this would increase any application size and render software development inefficient.

Many fundamental tasks, such as transmitting data packets or presenting text on a typical output screen, such as a monitor, may be delegated to system software, which acts as a bridge between hardware and software. System software allows applications to communicate with the devices predictably and consistently without even the applications' need to know specific details about the hardware.

The OS (Operating System) — can handle almost any range of applications if they all access the same services and resources in the same way. This decreases the time and programming needed to create and debug a program while making sure that users can monitor, manage, and manage system hardware across a standard and intuitive interface.

To optimize OS services to the particular hardware environment, the OS (Operating System) uses an extensive database of computer drivers. While any software may make an introductory call to the storage media, the OS receives the call and employs the associated driver to convert the call into commands required by the hardware resources on that computer. Nowadays, the OS (Operating System) serves as a robust interface for identifying, configuring, and managing various hardware, such as processors, processing modules, and memory management.

### Primary Functions of OS (Operating System):

An OS (Operating System) has three primary functions: it provides a user interface (UI) via a Command Line Interface (CLI) or a Graphical User Interface (GUI). It executes and regulates application execution, and defines and communicates system resources to such applications (typically via a structured API).

### User Interface (UI)

UI stands for the user interface. Every OS (Operating System) must have a graphical user interface (GUI), allowing users to communicate with the OS to set up, customize, and troubleshoot the OS and its hardware. CLI and GUI are the two main user interfaces available.

The CLI, also known as the terminal mode window, is a text-based system interface that allows users to enter commands, arguments, and parameters related to certain tasks using the standard keyboard. Individuals depend on inputs delivered by input devices such as touchscreens, touchpads, and mouse devices to navigate the GUI or desktop, which is based on icons and symbols.

Users who are mainly interested in modifying files and programs, like double-clicking an icon to open a file in its primary application, seem to be the most frequent GUI users. Professional developers and advanced users continue to favor the CLI as they must regularly manage extraordinarily rough and complex commands, such as developing and managing scripts to establish new computers for employees.

## Application Management

Every application is launched and managed by an OS (Operating System). This generally facilitates a range of behaviors, such as timesharing several processes, and threads, so different tasks can split the accessible processors' time. It also helps to manage disruptions that programs produce to get a processor's serious response. This helps to maintain there is enough capacity to run the program, and its data is presented without conflicting with other operations and performing errands.

An OS (Operating System) may also provide APIs that allow applications to use OS and hardware operations without understanding the limited OS or device state. A Windows API, for example, can help a software get input from a mouse and keyboard, build GUI elements like dialogue boxes and keys, read and write data to a storage device, and much more.

The OS on which an application is intended to run is usually customized. An OS can also provide various services to programs, namely:

- In a multi-user environment, where several programs will run simultaneously, the OS decides which programs should operate in what sequence and time each program should be given before moving on to the next.

- It manages I/O to and from connected hardware devices, including hard drives, printers, and dial-up interfaces.

- It sends notifications about the state of service and any failures that might have appeared to each program or system operator.

- It can handle batch job coordination so the facilitating application can focus on other tasks.

- An OS can handle how to split a program to run it on multiple processors simultaneously on systems that support parallel processing.

All main computer systems need an OS, and sometimes, an OS must be designed with multiple attributes to cater to different form factors.

## Device management

An OS is to define, customize, and connect computer devices to applications. The OS can configure device drivers. It recognizes and detects hardware, allowing the OS and programs to operate on the OS using the system without prior knowledge of the equipment or devices.

It is the OS (Operating System) responsibility to find the correct device and activate the driver software so a program only needs to make requests to the device and not have to use commands or codes unique to that device. Many devices, such as Connectivity options, communication ports, graphics devices like GPUs, motherboard chipsets, and even storage devices, are in a similar situation.

The OS (Operating System) recognizes and configures logical and physical devices for operation and usually stores them in a logical structure like the Windows Registry. To secure the proper system efficiency and protection, device makers must patch and upgrade drivers regularly, and the OS should do the same. The OS also downloads and modifies new drivers when computers are replaced.

## Types of Operating Systems:

Although an operating system's basic functions are similar, numerous operating systems cater to a wide multitude of platforms and user requirements.

## General Purpose OS:

This OS can be used for a variety of purposes. A general-purpose OS refers to a group of operating systems designed to run a wide range of applications on a wide range of hardware, allowing a user to run multiple applications or tasks simultaneously. A general-purpose operating system can be deployed on a variety of laptop and desktop configurations and run a variety of applications, including accounting software, directories, internet browsers, and games. To make sure that programs can efficiently share the broad range of hardware available, general-purpose OS usually concentrates on thread and hardware management.

The following are examples of popular desktop operating systems:

- The unofficial norm for office and home computers is Microsoft's signature operating system, Windows. The GUI-based operating system was first released in 1985 and has since been updated often.

- The OS for Apple's Mac line of computers and workstations is Mac OS.

- Unix is a multiple-user OS that focuses on adaptability and versatility. Unix was among the first OS to be developed in the C programming language, having been developed in the 1970s.

- Linux was created as a free alternative for PC users. Linux has a legacy for being a high-performing and reliable operating system.

## Mobile OS

Mobile operating systems cater to the specific requirements of mobile communication devices like tablets and smartphones. Compared to conventional PCs, mobile devices usually have minimal computational power, so the OS must also be scaled down in scale and complexity to reduce its resource consumption while maintaining enough resources for applications operating on the computer.

Mobile OS places a premium on advanced features, user accessibility, and data handling functions like streaming media. Mobile OS includes Google's Android and Apple's IOS.

### Embedded OS

Not all computers are multipurpose. Devices that need an OS can be used in a wide range of portable devices, like virtual home assistants, ATMs, aircraft systems, and the Internet - of - Things (IoT) systems. The main distinction is that the corresponding computing device just does one thing, so the operating system is scaled down and focused on efficiency and resilience. To keep operating in all situations, the OS should operate quickly, not malfunction, and elegantly manage all errors. Usually, the operating system is housed on a chipset that is built into the computer itself. An embedded OS, for instance, can be used in a medical system as part of a life support system and must function consistently to maintain the healthcare facility.

### Network Operating System.

A NOS is a customized operating system designed to make connectivity between devices on a local area network easier.

A network operating system (NOS) delivers the connectivity stack required to comprehend network protocols and build, exchange, and break down network packets. Since other OS types mostly manage network communication, a specialized NOS is essentially obsolete today.

### Real-Time Operating System

A real-time OS operates in real-time. The computer manufacturer may use a real-time OS when a computer system must communicate with the world within consistent and reproducible time constraints. An advanced manufacturing control system, for example, can guide the operations of a large factory or power station. A facility like this can generate signals from a variety of sensors and signal control valves, motors, and a variety of other devices. In these circumstances, the industrial management system must react rapidly and accurately to evolving realistic circumstances. Otherwise, tragedy may occur. Buffering, loading communication delays, and other pauses, which are reasonable in other forms of operating systems, are not allowed in an RTOS.

## 1.2 Linux as an Operating System

The Linux Kernel is the foundation for a group of open-source Unix-like operating systems. Linus Torvalds launched it for the first time in 1991. It is an open and free operating system, and the code can be updated and transferred to anyone for corporate or commercial purposes.

Linux is identical to several other operating systems you might have used in the past, such as Windows or Mac OS in several respects. Linux, among other operating systems, has a graphical user interface and the same software you are used to, such as text processors, picture editors, and video editing software. In certain instances, the developer of a program could have created a Linux version of the very same program you use on other platforms. Briefly, Linux can be used by anybody who can use a pc or laptop device.

However, Linux differs from other systems in several ways. Foremost, Linux is free and open-source software.

The source code for Linux is open source and free to download, update, and contribute to for anyone with the skills.

Linux is also unique in that, while the core components of Linux are widely available, there are several Linux distributions available, each with its own set of software alternatives. This indicates that Linux is adaptable, as not just programs like internet browsers and word processors can be replaced. Linux users can also customize key components such as the platform's visualization interface and other elements.

If you realize it or not, you are possibly still using Linux. Servers operating Linux create between one-third and two-thirds of all websites on the Internet, based on which consumer surveys you look at.

Individuals and companies prefer Linux for their databases because it is stable, scalable, and comes with great service from a wide user community.

Many devices you own run Linux, including Android phones, Chromebooks, electronic storage devices, portable video cameras, wearables, and more. Underneath the hood of your vehicle, Linux is operating. As part of the Operating System Framework for Linux, Microsoft Windows also includes Linux components.

Users who are unfamiliar with Linux often dismiss it, mistakenly believing it to be a complex and challenging operating system to use. Nevertheless, in recent years, Linux operating systems have become much more user-oriented than their Windows competitors are, so giving it a trial is the best way to determine if Linux is right for you.

### Advantages of Linux

- Linux's greatest benefit is that this is an open-source OS. This ensures that the source code is freely accessible to everyone and that you may contribute, change, and share the code with anyone.

- Linux is more stable than every operating system based on stability. This is not to say that Linux is secure. It does have vulnerabilities, but it is less prone than every other operating system. No anti-virus software is required.

- Linux updates are simple and regular.

- Numerous Linux distributions are available, which you can choose from based on your needs or preferences.

- Linux is a free operating system that can be downloaded from the Internet.

- It has a sizable following in the community.

- It has a high level of stability. It hardly halts or crashes, and it need not be rebooted after a short period.

- It protects the users' privacy.

- The efficiency of the Linux operating system is better than those of other operating systems. It enables a significant proportion of individuals to perform all the tasks and effectively manages them.

- It is suitable for use on a network.

- Linux has a lot of versatility. You do not have to install the entire Linux suite. You only need to install the components required.

- Linux can read and write a wide range of file formats.

- Installing it from the web is quick and easy. It can be installed on any hardware, including your old computer.

- Even if the hard disc space is limited, it completes all tasks correctly.

## 1.3 From UNIX to Linux

The Linux operating system is ideal for small to medium-sized businesses, and it is now often used in large corporations where UNIX was originally the only choice. Linux was once thought to be an interesting research project. Most large organizations, where networking and multi-user communication were the primary concerns, did not see Linux as a choice. However, with significant software companies transferring their software to Linux and the OS's ability to be widely distributed, it has become a viable choice for Web hosting and business applications.

However, there are situations where UNIX is or was the immediate solution. If a company used huge symmetric multiprocessing programs or structures with even over eight CPUs, it had to operate UNIX. UNIX was much more powerful than Linux at efficiently managing all operations. However, since 2004, Linux has been used on more of the world's largest supercomputers than UNIX.

Since Linux is an open-source operating system, it can be provided free. Anybody can obtain a copy of Linux from magazines, publications, or the Internet. Organizations usually pay vendors for a service contract rather than the software for server versions. The major server equipment manufacturers are IBM, Hp, and Dell.

UNIX is more expensive than Linux. Medium-range UNIX servers cost somewhere around $25,000 to $249,999. HP, SUN, and IBM are the main distributors. A top-of-the-line UNIX server will cost upwards of $500,000. IBM is the leading company in UNIX servers, as per IDC and Gartner, with HP in second place and SUN in seventh.

Commercial UNIX is normally tailored for each system, resulting in a high initial cost, while Linux has model packages. Linux has a model that is more similar to Windows than just a corporate UNIX OS. Users who buy a UNIX server get a Supplier assistance package that includes help setting up and maintaining the system. Vendor support must be bought separately with Linux.

Both operating devices are prone to viruses, but Linux is much more equipped to deal with them. Most of the same features and functions present in UNIX were implemented into Linux, along with user domain classification in multi-user environments, task separation in multi-tasking environments, a code mechanism that can be authenticated and/or accessed remotely, and so much more. Since Linux is an open-source operating system, anybody can address bugs in the consumer forum, and they can be patched within days. However, that is not the situation for UNIX, and the user must wait for a long time to receive the correct bug-fixing patch. Since it does not go through the lengthy development processes of corporate operating systems, the developer community usually delivers updates sooner.

At the same point, Linux is funded by thousands of developers as an open-source operating system. To clarify, this enables for more creativity and faster time-to-market features than UNIX can offer.

Over the last few years, Linux has evolved quicker than any server operating system. According to estimates, there are over 25 million Linux devices in use, contrary to 5.5 million UNIX systems.

Linux is growing rapidly due to its use in embedded technology, and its free and easy availability. To cope with Linux, companies like HP, IBM, and SUN are developing customized UNIX systems with graphical user interfaces and user-friendly interfaces also Linux compliant.

## 1.4 Systems Architecture of Linux

The kernel is a part of the OS that manages the CPU resources, distributes memory, transmits data, schedules processes, executes applications, and keeps them safe from one another. When the computer boots up, the first application is loaded. The kernel's most important pieces of code are mounted into secure memory areas to prevent them from being overwritten by certain operating system applications.

Linux is an operating system that can be implemented on a wide range of hardware and used to build software, run programs, and more. The kernel is at the core of Linux. Linux was originally written in C language to run on i386 machines but has since been adapted to more devices than every other operating system. Linux is now the most widely used operating system on the planet.

A CLI (Command Line Interface), also described as a shell, is used to manage Linux. Linux distributions provide a range of Linux applications, such as application software for managing and operating hardware, shared libraries, programs, and system tasks, which run simultaneously and refer to network requests, besides the kernel, which manages software and hardware processes. For Linux, there are over 70,000 programs to choose from, and a variety of programming languages. Packages that comprise both the application and information about it are used to install applications.

It is necessary to understand that all operating systems run their binaries in kernel space to prevent the kernel from suspending and disrupting the system. Whenever a user accesses a program or method, it runs in userspace. This differentiation is important. Applications may originate from a range of places, be underdeveloped, or come from unidentified sources. These programs cannot tamper with kernel infrastructure and trigger the system to malfunction because they are running outside of kernel space.

To connect system memory resources or network equipment, all programs, including system daemon tasks that perform essential operating system tasks, must make a system request to the kernel. Every professional multi-operating system does have a user-space vs. kernel space configuration created to keep it safe, quick, and dependable.

In a nutshell, the separation of kernel space and the user makes Linux the most stable and safe operating system possible.

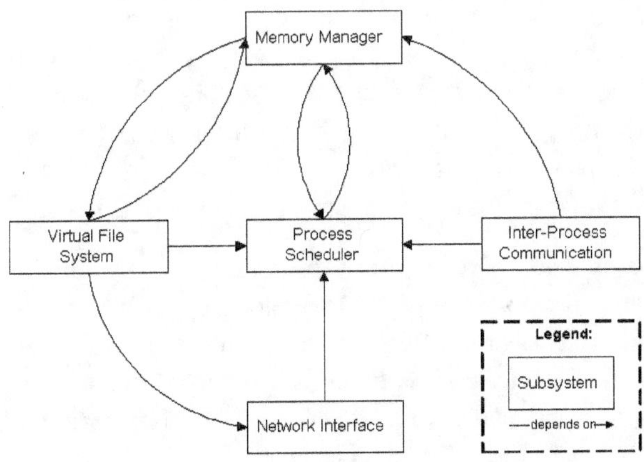

The process scheduler would be the most important subsystem. All other components depend on it because they all need to pause and restart processes.

Typically, a subsystem will pause a program awaiting the completion of a device operation and restart the process once the process is done. When a process tries to deliver a message throughout the network, the network interface can pause the process before the device has successfully sent the request. The network interface, therefore, restores the procedure with a return code showing the outcome of the operation after the request has been received (or the device has returned a failure).
For similar purposes, the process scheduler, virtual database server, and inter-process coordination all rely on the process scheduler.

The following are some of the less evident but crucially significant dependencies:

- When an operation is restored, the memory manager is used by the process-scheduler interface to update the hardware data map for that process.

- The memory manager is required by the inter-process processing subsystem to enable shared-memory network communication. This method enables two processes to use a shared memory area with their memory.

- The network interface is used by the virtual file system to aid a network file system (NFS), and the memory controller is used to provide the ramdisk unit.

- The digital file system is used by the memory manager to facilitate switching. It is the only factor why the memory manager is dependent mostly on the process scheduler. Whenever a process attempts to access swapped-out information, the memory manager sends a request to the system files to retrieve the memory from permanent storage, and the process is halted.

- Compared to the explicit constraints, all modules in the kernel depend on a certain common infrastructure that is not visible in either subsystem. Both kernel components use these protocols to assign and free resources for the kernel's use, and procedures to print alert or error alerts, and system monitoring routines. These tools will not be listed directly since they are believed to be widely accessible.

- At this stage, the architectural design reflects that of Garlan and Shaw's Data Abstraction style. Each one of the portrayed subsystems comprises state information that can be accessed through a procedural framework, and each subsystem is ultimately in control of the resources it manages.

The Linux kernel's technical framework is successful. Key factors in this performance were the arrangement for developer organization and system configurability.

To maintain a large number of individual volunteer programmers, the Linux kernel framework was needed. This criterion proposed that the platform's most development-intensive components, such as hardware application software and file and networking interfaces, could be incorporated powerfully and flexibly.

The Linux designer chose an application and database method to make these structures flexible. Each physical domain controller is configured as a separate segment with a shared interface. In this manner, a single developer could introduce a new system driver with little interaction from other Linux kernel developers. The success of a significant number of professional developers in implementing the kernel demonstrates the feasibility of this technique.

Including more compatible hardware platforms in a Linux kernel is another significant enhancement. The system's architecture encourages extensibility by breaking down all equipment code into separate modules in each module.

By re-designing only the device parts of the kernel, a few developers can port the Linux kernel to something like a major hardware framework.

## 1.5 File Hierarchy Structure of Linux

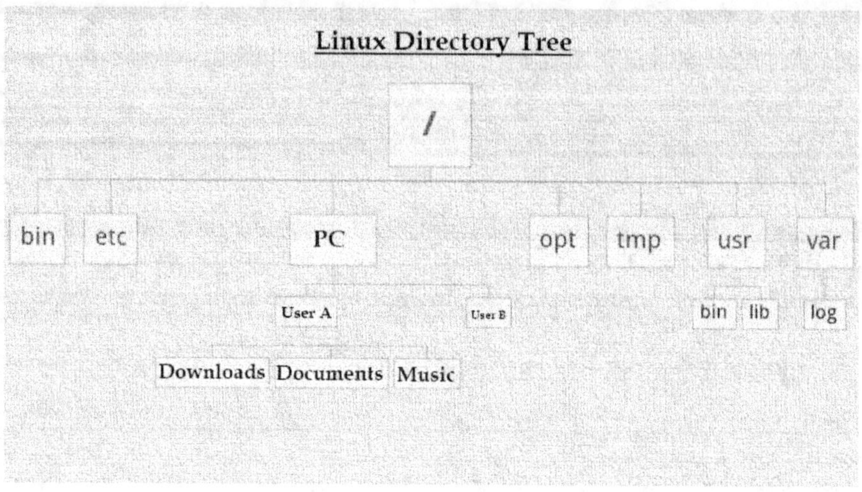



The directory configuration in Linux is similar to that of a tree. The root of the Linux system file structure is where it all starts. All begin at the base, but directories expand off it.

In Linux, a forward slash (/) is used to separate directories. "Forward slash" is called "slash" when discussing files and directory routes. Since the complete reference to it is /, the system files' origin is often linked to as "slash." The origin directory is referred to when someone says, "check-in slash" or "the directory is in slash."

Executable or binary files are found in the /bin directory. Applications are developed in source code, which is plain text that individuals can interpret. After that, the data is processed into machine-readable binaries. Computer code is a sequence of zeros and ones, so they are called binaries. The most important thing to remember is that functions, applications, and programs can often be found in /bin.

The /etc. the directory contains configuration files. Configuration files regulate the behavior of the operating system and applications. For example, a file in /etc., for example, instructs the operating system to either boot into the graphic mode or text mode.

## 1.6 The Process Architecture of Linux

Inside the operating system, processes perform the tasks. Software is machine language data and instruction in an interactive image on a disc. A process is a software program in motion.

It is a complex object continuously evolving as the processor executes machine code commands. The process contains the program counter, including all the CPU's logs and the process frames, including temporary files such as task parameters, return links, saved quantities, and the program's data and instructions. The current operation in the processor is included in the executing program or method. Linux is an operating system that supports multiple processors. Processes are specific activities with their own set of rights and obligations.

When one process fails, it does not affect other processes in the system. Each process has its virtual memory and can only communicate with other processes via stable, kernel-managed frameworks.

A process can consume a lot of system resources throughout its existence. It will operate its commands on the device's CPUs and store itself and its data in the system's memory space. It can open and use files inside the file servers and use the electronic components in the process explicitly or implicitly.

Linux can keep a record of the process and the device resources available to it to handle the other operations in the system equally. If one process constrained much of the system's memory space or CPUs, it would be unfair to other operations in the system.

The CPU is the most valuable resource in the system, and there is typically only one. Linux is a multitasking operating system that runs a process from each CPU throughout the system at all points of time to optimize CPU utilization.

When there are more operations than CPUs, the remaining processes should wait for a Processor to become available before they can function. Multiprocessing is a straightforward process. A process runs until it needs to wait for something, usually a system resource. Once it has that resource, it can run again. The CPU may remain idle in a unit-processing framework, such as DOS, and the waiting period would be wasted. Many processes are stored in memory at one time in a multiprocessing system.

When a process is forced to wait, the OS shifts the CPU from that operation to another, more worthy process. The scheduler determines which operation is the most suitable to run immediately, and Linux employs a variety of scheduling techniques to ensure consistency. Linux supports various binary file formats, including ELF & Java, which must be handled equitably.

Linux facilitates real-time processes in addition to standard processes. These processes must respond to external factors rapidly, and the scheduler treats them differently than regular user processes. Even though the task struct system architecture is diverse and complicated, its domains can be separated into several functional departments:

**State:**

A process's condition varies as it operates, depending on the situation. The following are the phases of Linux processes:

**Running:**

The program has either been operating (it is the system's present process) or prepared to run (it is awaiting assignment to one of the device's CPUs).

**Waiting:**

The process is preparing the occurrence of an incident or the availability of a resource. Linux distinguishes between time-limited and uninterruptible waiting processes. Signals can disrupt interruptible working processes, while uninterruptible working processes depend on hardware parameters and cannot be disrupted under any conditions.

**Stopped:**

The phase has come to a halt, generally because of receiving signals. A reimplemented process can be on hold.

**Zombie:**

This is a stopped process with a task struct data model in the process vector for some cause. It is precisely what it looks like: a dormant procedure.

**Scheduling Data:**

This data is obtained by the scheduler in particular for it to reasonably determine which operation in the system needs to run.

**Identifiers:**

A process identifier is assigned to each process in the system.
A process identifier is just a number, not an iterator, into the process vector. Each process often has user and group identifiers, which are used to restrict access to the platform's files and equipment.

# CHAPTER 2
# DECIDE YOUR DISTRIBUTION

Linux distributions implement open-source code into a single platform that can then be mounted and booted. Linux distributions are also available for personal computers, non-graphical servers, server farms, handheld devices, and special applications such as home theatre Computers and embedded systems. Anyone may build their latest Linux distribution by building it from source code or changing an existing distribution since it is open-source software. Over 300 Linux distributions are kept and maintained at the moment.

## 2.1 What is a Linux Distribution?

A Linux distribution, also known as a Linux Distro, is a computer operating system made up of components created by different open-source developers and software developers. The Linux kernel, the GNU shell utilities, the desktop environment, the X server, an installer, a package management system, and other resources are all included with each distribution. Many elements are created independently of one another and distributed as source code. A web browser, productivity tools, and other applications, like the KVM hypervisor, are also included in most distributions. Vast numbers of software applications, utilities, and programs can be included in a single Linux distribution.

A distribution is an entirely composed Linux system kit.
A Linux distribution includes the GNU project tools, the Linux kernel, and a variety of open-source application projects that add to the system's capabilities.

There are various Linux distributions available to satisfy almost every computing need. The majority of Linux distributions are tailored to a particular user community, such as corporate customers, media hobbyists, computer programmers, or regular end-users.

Each personalized distribution comes with the software needed to support specialized functions, like video and audio production software for multimedia professionals or decoders and integrated development environments for application developers.

The Linux distributions are most often classified into three groups:

- Specialized distributions

- Core distributions

- Live test distributions

The subsequent sections explain the categories of Linux distributions and provide Linux distro instances in each group.


## Core Distributions

A core distribution includes the GNU and Linux operating systems, one and sometimes more visual desktop interfaces, and nearly any Linux program available, which are ready to install and use. No matter your needs, the core Linux distribution offers one-stop convenience for a comprehensive Linux configuration.

A distribution was published as floppy discs in the initial periods of Linux. You had to import classes of items and copy those onto discs manually. A whole distribution will typically need 20 or even more discs. This was, without a doubt, a traumatic experience.

As DVD or CD players became more popular in personal computers, Linux distributions became available as a CD set or a separate DVD. Typically, you can download a standard DVD image file (also known as an ISO file because of the file extension) and then mount that image to a DVD. It was a lot easier to install Linux after that.

| Distribution | Description |
| --- | --- |
| Slackware | One of the original Linux distribution sets, popular with Linux geeks |
| Red Hat | A commercial business distribution used mainly for servers |
| CentOS | The open source version of Red Hat designed for testing |
| Fedora | Another open source version of Red Hat, but designed for home use |
| Gentoo | A distribution designed for advanced Linux users, containing only Linux source code |
| SUSE | A commercial distribution for business use |
| Debian | Popular with Linux experts and commercial Linux products |

Linux distributions are still distributed as ISO image files. Many computers no longer have DVD players, and utilities enable you to mount them onto a bootable flash drive. New computers can boot from USB drives, which are still widely found on both servers and workstations.

While getting many choices in distribution is perfect for Linux experts, newcomers can challenge it. During the setup process, most kernels ask questions to decide which programs should be loaded by default, what devices are linked to the computer, and how to enable the hardware. These issues can be perplexing for newcomers.

They frequently either load far too many programs on their machine or load little, only to find later that their system is incapable of performing the tasks they need.

## Specialized Distributions

Over time, a new subset of distributions emerged, aimed directly at new Computer users. These are based primarily on core distributions but only include a handful of software appropriate for a particular use case.

Apart from offering tailored applications (such as office items for corporate customers), customized Linux distributions often try to assist new Linux users by automatically detecting and setting up popular hardware devices. This makes downloading and installing Linux even more convenient.

| Distribution | Description |
| --- | --- |
| Mint | A desktop distribution configured to replace a standard Windows workstation |
| Ubuntu | Provides desktop and server distributions designed for school and home use |
| MX Linux | A desktop distribution for home users with older hardware |
| openSUSE | An open source version of the commercial SUSE distribution |
| PCLinuxOS | A distribution focusing on support for advanced graphics and sound cards |
| Puppy | Another small distribution that runs well on older PCs |

## Live Test Distributions

The bootable DVD Linux distribution, also known as Lived, has been a massive hit in the Linux field. Most computers nowadays allow you to boot up by accessing the OS from a Disc or Thumb drive rather than the hard disk drive. This allows you to get a feel for a Linux system without having to install it.

Many Linux distributions build a bootable ISO image you can mount to a Disc or USB to enjoy this functionality's benefits. These distributions only have a portion of the Linux system.

The demo can not contain a full Linux system owing to space constraints, but you would be shocked at how much functionality they can pack in! You can load your computer from a USB stick and afterward download the remaining packages from the Web.

This is a great way to try out different Linux distributions, all without having to touch your computer. Insert a DVD, and you are ready to go. All Linux software can be run directly from a DVD or USB drive. Almost every distribution now has a Live version, making it simple to download one from the distribution and burn it to a DVD to try out.

Some Live distributions, like Ubuntu, also enable you to run the Linux distribution from its Live device. This allows you to boot from a disc or USB drive, try out the distribution, and afterward deploy it on your computer system if you like it. This is a very convenient and consumer-friendly feature.

Linux Live distributions, like all good stuff, have a few flaws. Since everything is accessed via the USB or CD / DVD, programs run slower, mainly if you are using outdated computers with slower Optical drives. Additionally, any improvements you introduce to the system will be lost when you reboot.

## 2.2 How to choose the right distribution for you?

The best Linux distribution for you is determined by your usage scenario and tool specifications. For various purposes, different Linux distributions are preferable. Some distributions are made for desktop use, while others are made to help backend IT frameworks.

If you are looking for a new Linux distribution, the first thing you can think about is whether you require an enterprise Linux distribution or perhaps a community Linux distribution.

Linux distributions come in various varieties: community and enterprise. A community distribution is a widespread Linux distribution mostly supported and funded by an open-source network. An enterprise Linux distribution, also known as a commercial distro, is available via a vendor membership and therefore does not depend exclusively on the community's support.

The main distinction between group and enterprise distributions is just who determines what matters to consumers. Contributors select and manage packages from a broad range of open-source choices, determining a group distro course. A distributor determines the course of an enterprise distribution based on the consumers.

**<u>Factors to Consider While Choosing a Distribution</u>**

**<u>General-Purpose Software</u>** - (Prog. Languages, Office Apps, Graphics software, Games, etc.). Many distributions are minimal and have little software. Some distributions are the polar opposite. This all varies depending on your requirements as a customer. If the application is not pre-bundled, you can usually download it without difficulty.

<u>Cost</u> – whether or not you pay zero, a little or a considerable amount for distribution is determined by your needs and the distributor's operating model. Many commercial distributions provide corporate support.

They provide telephone helplines and round-the-clock support for companies that depend on Linux systems for anything from basic needs to project requirements.

It is worth noting, though, that even though you pay for the application, it does not imply that it is better. You are paying for things like licenses, paperwork, salaried personnel, end-user functionality updates, and customer service.

<u>Installation Software</u> – Alternative techniques of 'packaging up' applications are used for different distributions. APT is used by Debian-based systems such as Linux Mint and Ubuntu. While this is mostly meaningless these days, they still operate in somewhat nuanced ways.

<u>Latest Updates</u> – Many distributions are not updated for months or years. They may anticipate the version to be 'stable,' thus providing no updates until there is a significant security patch or are prepared to upgrade. Some distributions, usually the more specialized ones, often end and close.

<u>Support</u> – Most of the more popular distros have excellent community assistance in message boards or messaging channels. Some still have free Linux programs and configuration, but you can also sign up for a service contract.

<u>Ease of Use</u> – How easy it is to use an OS also accounts for a factor while choosing a distribution.

## 2.3 Ubuntu

Ubuntu is now one of the most widely used Linux distributions.
It is based on Debian, but it has a more consistent release schedule. It is more refined than Debian, simpler to use, and has a lot of money behind it.

Since Ubuntu is a free operating system, proprietary resources such as MP3 player "codecs" are not included by default. Therefore, download them separately, which is a simple process. Advantages of Ubuntu:

- Simple to use

- A unique consumer experience

- The software center has an extensive range of software programs.

- Pre-installed essential tools

Canonical, the organization that created and supports Ubuntu, also provides enterprise-level support for the operating system. Desktop, Server, and Core are the three major models. Other 'spins' include Edubuntu, Lubuntu, Kubuntu, and others, created with public education in mind. There have been around 40 third-party spins in existence today in addition to the authorized spins.

Ubuntu comes out twice per year. The April update includes a 'Long Term Support' update every two years. These come with five years of free help. This comprises bug fixes and protection updates. Normal 'intermediation' releases come with a nine-month support period, but updating one version to the next is straightforward.

If you do not like the Ubuntu interface, Linux Mint is built on Ubuntu, is designed for beginners, and includes GNOME, Cinnamon, and KDE, versions. Linux Mint is somewhat identical to Ubuntu in terms of functionality.

## 2.4 Linux Mint

Linux Mint is, without a doubt, the finest Ubuntu-based distribution for newcomers. Yes, it is built on Ubuntu. You can expect the benefits that come with Ubuntu. It does, however, deliver a variety of workspace environments, including MATE, Cinnamon, and Xfce, instead of the GNOME platform. In reality, Linux Mint outperforms Ubuntu in a few other areas.

It is not just about the typical user experience, which is a plus for Windows operating systems. It offers excellent productivity with limited technical specifications, mainly when used with the MATE or Xfce desktop environments.

It also makes use of Ubuntu's application repositories.

You would not have to be concerned about software installation.

Mint 20 comes in three desktop versions: MATE, Cinnamon, and XFCE. It is centered on Ubuntu 20.04 LTS. Mint no longer supports 32-bit variants, and only 64-bit editions are available. Linux Mint 20 is based upon Linux kernel 5.4, which includes enhanced compatibility for NVIDIA GPUs, AMD Navi 12, and Intel CPUs. The overall user interface has also been updated, with new icons, new styles, and a digitally enhanced taskbar.

Warpinator, a file-sharing software that operates in a LAN, and a fractional scaling function for HiDPI monitors to experience clearer and crisper images are among the new features. Firefox, Timeshift, Audacious music player, LibreOffice, Timeshift, and Thunderbird are among the other applications.

Linux Mint is a fantastic Windows-like operating distribution. So, if you do not want a specific user experience, Linux Mint is a good option.

## 2.5 MX Linux

It is creating a community of devoted users from both the antiX and MEPIS communities working together. The aim is to create a mid-weight, convenient Linux distribution that combines both environments' best features.

The most recent version (MX 17.1) is available with either 32-bit or 64-bit architectures from the MX website. There is already a more positive thing: about the current release ISO files, regular updates are downloadable. These are brand-new ISO images, including the latest improvements installed, so you will not have to waste time upgrading after a new install.

Instead of the more prevalent Mint (LMDE) or Calamares installers, MX Linux nevertheless uses its own.

The platform is Xfce 4.12, but it has a well-thought-out and straightforward setup. Our preference is for the panel to be on the left of the screen. This enables the optimum use of the available screen. The panel is not set to auto-hide, which most people prefer on their laptops with smaller screens. No problem, right-click the window, go to Panel, then Preferences, and pick auto-hide from the menu.

It has Conky operating in the backgrounds that provide day/date/load details, but there is still a Conky Switch function in the favorites menu if you do not want it.

In the menu favorites, there is also an MX Tools utility. This reminds us of MEPIS, a useful, user-friendly utility that allows you to control a wide range of system settings.

There are a few exclusive features here you will not find on other platforms. For fine-tuning your system, the Tweak and Conky config utilities are handy.

Drivers (Nvidia) and codecs can also be installed, and there is another MX-specific development kit for those who do not want to struggle with the Synaptic command line.

## 2.6 Open SUSE

SuSE used to be a stand-alone Linux distribution that Novell later bought out. Micro Focus then bought that out. They have been bought and sold often since then and now have a total value of about $USD 2.5 billion.

SUSE Leap is a milestone release that addresses computer users and corporate design and deployment.

The OpenSUSE initiative is a progressive and robust collaboration program that provides two key SUSE subsidiaries: SUSE Enterprise and SUSE Leap. It is suitable among open-source programmers and data administrators.

On the other hand, SUSE Tumbleweed is a rolling update that includes the most up-to-date software frames and IDEs. Thanks to the emergence of up-to-date bundles such as office programs, the GCC interpreter, and the kernel, TumbleWeed is a lot easier for every power user or computer programmer.

OpenSUSE depends on the Yast package manager, which is preferred for programmers and software operators for handling software applications.

SuSE, like RedHat, has a complete business version and a production version. SuSE is an excellent all-arounder oriented toward the enterprise, with sponsorship and corporate collaborations with companies like SAP. Red Hat and SUSE share more than just the corporate system. It was initially based on Red Hat and hence used the same RPM-based package control system, but it has evolved enough to be considered a distribution with its liberties. Its YAST management information system makes service setup easy.

OpenSuSE is the name of SuSE's free edition. OpenSuSE has several exclusive features, namely Tumbleweed, a cutting-edge application software system. Several developer tools are included, such as openQA, which is designed for interactive software development, and Kiwi, which generates Linux visuals for installation on actual devices. By default, OpenSUSE utilizes the KDE desktop.

## 2.7 Fedora

Fedora has long been regarded as among the leading user-friendly operating systems, thanks to its ease of use and pre-installed applications that help beginners get up and running quickly.

It is a robust and adaptable operating system designed for desktop computers and notebooks, servers, and even IoT environments. Fedora is built on Red Hat and serves as a testing ground for the company before moving into the Enterprise process.

It is typically used for creation and education, and it is useful for both programmers and learners. Fedora has been using the DNF package for a long time (and it is still the standard package manager) and provides the most up-to-date and best RPM software applications. Fedora 32 is the most recent version of Fedora.

## 2.8 Debian

Debian is known for giving rise to well-known Linux distributions like Mint, Deepin, and Ubuntu,  which have delivered outstanding results, reliability, and user interface. Debian 10.5, an upgrade to Debian 10 recognized as Debian Buster, is the most recent stable version.

Debian 10.5 is not the latest iteration of Debian Buster. Instead, it is an upgrade to Buster, including the most recent enhancements and new application software. Security patches that resolve pre-existing vulnerabilities are included. There is no reason to get rid of the Buster system if you already have one. Use the APT development kit to update your system.

The Debian initiative has over 59,000 development tools and supports a wide variety of computers, with each version covering a wider variety of system configurations. It aims for cutting-edge innovation and long-term sustainability. Secure, Research, and Volatile are the three main development divisions in Debian.

As its name implies, the stable version is rock-solid and comes with maximum security protection but does not come with the most up-to-date software programs. It is, however, suitable for web servers due to its reliability and quality, and it also qualifies for more moderate computer users who are not concerned with providing the most up-to-date software programs. Debian Stable is the default system on most systems.

Debian Testing is a continuous update that contains the most up-to-date software not yet integrated further into a stable release. This is the subsequent stable Debian release's development phase. It usually is prone to instabilities and is easily broken. It also does not receive security updates promptly. Bullseye is the most recent Debian Testing release.

Debian's unstable distribution is still in active development. It is an innovative distribution that serves as an ideal forum for programmers who actively contribute to the code before it reaches the 'Testing' level.

Millions of people are using Debian because of its extensive package repositories and its reliability, particularly in production systems.

## 2.9 Arch Linux

Arch Linux is a quirky Linux distribution compact and portable intended for experienced users or Linux specialists concerned with what is mounted and operating. It allows users to customize or configure the system according to their preferences. Arch is designed for people who are well-versed in the workings of Linux.

Unlike most Linux distributions, Arch Linux is not generated from a parental distribution such as Debian or Red Hat. Since it is built on a primary (yet stable) foundation, it remains alone and is respected by techies for lightning-fast Linux distribution. All else is added via the Pacman packaging process

Arch is a continuous release, which means it is all updated. All you must do is refresh the modules in the interface. The standard package administrator is Pacman, and it makes use of the Arch User Repository, which is a platform for installing software programs. The most recent update is 2020.09.01.

## 2.10 Slackware

Starting in 1993, Slackware was most likely the first accurate Linux distribution. It employss.tar.gz packages instead of the more familiar YUM or APT frameworks, identical to Arch.If you are a more experienced user who doesn't want to compile anything, Arch might be for you, as it still allows for equal rates of customization as Slackware.

Slackware, centered mostly on Soft-landing Linux Distribution, has served as the foundation for several other Software packages, most prominently the first variants of SUSE Linux distros, and is the earliest still-maintained release.

Slackware strives to be a much more "Unix-like" distribution by focusing on design reliability and convenience.

It attempts not to predict usage cases or exclude consumer decisions by making a few changes appropriate to application packages from upwards. Unlike most mainstream Linux distributions, Slackware lacks a visual setup process and does not automatically resolve application software dependencies. For setup and management, it relies on text files and a few shell scripts.

It boots into something like a command-line control environment with no further modification. Slackware is also thought to be best suited for experienced and professionally oriented Linux users due to its many restrictive and straightforward features.

Although Slackware is open-source software and free, it lacks a structured bug-tracking system or community code repository, mostly with Volkerding announcing updates regularly. Developers do not have a structured membership process, and Volkerding seems to be the main contributor to launches.

## 2.11 Gentoo

Gentoo is just a distro designed for specialists who recognize the services they are dealing with right from the start. Developers, frameworks, and network engineers fall under this group. It is not recommended for Linux newbies. Gentoo is intended for those who seek a greater comprehension of the Linux-based operating system's pros and cons.

Gentoo comes with portage, a package control system used in other distros, including Calculate Linux and Sabayon, centered upon Gentoo and compatible with it. It is written in Python and is built on the principle of port collections. BSD-based distributions such as NetBSD and OpenBSD include port collections, which are compilations of updates and patches.

## 2.12 CentOS

The CentOS Platform is a public operating system created and developed by the CentOS group to provide a secure and stable open-source environment.

CentOS, which is focused on RHEL and is available for free download and update, is an excellent substitute to Red Hat Linux.

It provides users with RHEL's reliability and accuracy while also providing them with free protection and functionality improvements. CentOS 8 is a popular option among Linux users who want to take advantage of RHEL's features.

CentOS 8.2 is the most recent edition, and it is the third version of CentOS 8. It uses BaseOS and App stream repositories and comes pre-installed with the most recent software packages, like Python 3.8, Maven 3.6, GCC 9.1, and so on.

# CHAPTER 3
# INSTALL LINUX

Instead of Linux, Microsoft Windows comes preloaded on the majority of today's PCs. While this approach makes devices convenient to use out of the general public package, it also implies that you will almost always have to mount it yourself if you use Linux.

In the initial periods of Linux, getting Linux to operate on a PC required almost a bachelor's degree in computer science. Interestingly for us, graphical installations are now relatively simple to complete and would be recognizable to users who have used a graphical OS like Microsoft Windows. This chapter covers everything you need to know about installing and running a Linux distribution on your computer.

Even though various Linux distributions utilize multiple installer commands, they are all brilliant. Although you might not see practically the same visuals as we do in the installment, the basic principles should be similar. Do not be alarmed if you notice something new or one we have not mentioned. The installer is merely tailoring what it provides to your computer system and the applications you want to update.

## 3.1 What Is a Virtual Machine?

A virtual machine application generates a virtualized ecosystem known as a virtual machine that acts as a standalone computer system, mostly using virtual hardware systems. On your existing operating system, the VM operates as just a process in a window. You may use a virtual machine to boot an OS installer disc, and the operating system would be enticed into believing it is operating on a real device. This will mount and operate in the same way as it does on a physical computer. You can launch the virtual machine software to use it in a browser on your existing desktop anytime you run the operating system.

Virtual machines enable users to operate an OS in even a Windows app that acts as a separate device. You can utilize them to experiment with multiple operating systems, run applications that your primary operating system does not support, and test applications in a secure, virtualized framework.

The default system software on your machine is called the host while operating systems working within VMs are guests. It keeps things from being too perplexing.

The guest OS is mounted on a digital hard drive in a specific VM. This file is presented to the guest OS by the VM app as a regular hard drive. This ensures that you did not have to deal with segmentation or something else tricky with your physical hard drive.

Since virtualization introduces overhead, do not presume them to run as quickly as they would if you mounted the interface on actual devices. Virtual machines do not work well with challenging games or other applications that need a lot of visuals and Processor speed, so they are not the best way to run Windows games on Mac OS X or Linux not unless they are old or not graphically intense.

Companies introduced server virtualization to better use their physical servers' processing resources, reducing the necessity for server farms and saving resources in the data center. VMs, as we recognize them today, grew in popularity over the last 15 years. Independent server hardware was not needed for each app since it could operate on a single specific host with various OS specifications.

There can be two types of virtual machines: process virtual machines, which isolate a single function, and virtual system machines, which isolate the application or system from the computer system. The NET Framework, the Java virtual machine, and the Parrot virtual machine process virtual machines.

Hypervisors are used by system VMs as a middleman, allowing software to access system resources. Intel/Linux Foundation (Xen),  VMware (ESX/ESXi), Oracle (Oracle VM Server for x86 and MV Server for SPARC ), and Microsoft are all top players in the hypervisor domain (Hyper-V).

Digital machines can be used on desktop computers. A Mac user using a virtual Windows 10 version on their actual Mac hardware is the most obvious example.

**Practical Uses of Virtual Machines:**

Virtual Machines can be used for multiple. Some are listed below:

<u>Experiment with different platforms</u>: Installing different Linux distributions across a virtual machine allows you to try them out and learn how they operate. Operating macOS on Windows 10 inside a virtual machine allows you to familiarise yourself with various operating systems you may want to use full-time.

<u>Consolidate servers</u>: Businesses with multiple servers can virtualize some servers and execute them on a single device. Because each VM is a self-contained compartment, it avoids the security issues that come with running multiple servers on the same OS. Virtual machines could also be relocated from one physical server to another.

<u>Use apps that demand an old operating system</u>: If users' critical application requires Windows XP, users can run it in a virtual machine with XP installed. This enables users to use the software only compatible with Windows XP without having to install it. This is significant because Microsoft no longer supports Windows XP.

<u>Test applications on different platforms</u>: You can download each operating system in a VM to evaluate how an application performs on multiple platforms.

<u>Use software created for a different operating system</u>: Users of Linux and Mac os can run Windows in a VM to run Windows applications on their desktops without worrying about compatibility issues. Games, regrettably, are an issue. Virtual machine systems add overhead, and 3D games in a VM would not run smoothly.

People can execute multiple OS implementations on a specific device since the program is segregated from the actual host computer, improving efficiency, financing costs, and physical space. Another benefit of virtual machines is that they can run legacy applications, diminishing or reducing the need for and expense of transferring an outdated app to a newer operating system.

Developers use virtual machines (VMs) to test applications in a secure, virtualized environment. It can also aid in the isolation of ransomware that can infect a specific VM case. As malicious software within a VM cannot interact with the host system, it cannot do as much harm.

There are a few drawbacks to Virtual machines. Running multiple virtual machines on a single physical host can cause performance issues, particularly if the architecture specifications for a specific application are not met. Although particularly compared to a computer system, this renders them less powerful. The majority of IT operations use a mix of virtual and physical structures.

Virtualization software is the key to operating databases in virtual machines. Virtualization software comes in a variety of options. The most common in the Linux sector are:

- **KVM**: It is an open-source initiative that integrates with the Linux kernel directly. It can only run on systems with a virtualization-capable CPU.

- **VirtualBox**: An Oracle-sponsored project that installs in any Linux distribution, regardless of kernel or CPU type.

- **VMware Server:** It is a software package offered by VMware that runs on Windows, Mac OS X, and Linux hosts and is available in both free and commercial versions.

These virtualization software bundles install on a Linux host and allow users to simultaneously access multiple virtual network operating systems, like Linux and Windows.

In this chapter, we will show you how to set up and use Oracle VirtualBox and how to run a Linux workspace as a virtual machine.


**Installing a Virtual Machine:**

The first move is to install VirtualBox. This bundle may be available in the distribution software repository, depending on your Linux distribution. The VirtualBox software kit is included in the standard software repositories for both Ubuntu and OpenSUSE.

Install it on your device using the Ubuntu Software program or the openSUSE Software Center. The package appears in the device launcher after it has been installed.

If your Linux distribution does not include VirtualBox, or if you just want to make sure you have the most recent update, you can get it directly from the VirtualBox website and install it from there. VirtualBox's website has installation packages for several popular Linux distributions (including Ubuntu and OpenSUSE). It is critical to choose the correct VirtualBox version for your Linux distribution while downloading the program.

The processes to download and install the VirtualBox kit from the website are:

1.  Go to http://www.virtualbox.org in a web browser.

    - Even though Oracle sponsors the VirtualBox project, it has its website with download files, documentation, and a community forum.

2.  Click the Downloads tab on the main web page, on the left-hand side.

3.  Determine the Linux platform's latest VirtualBox edition.

    - This applies to the host site you have chosen. Other operating systems, like Microsoft Windows, can also be run inside the VirtualBox program.

    - VirtualBox is available for both Microsoft Windows and Apple's Mac OS X. If you are nervous about installing Linux on an existing Windows or Mac system, you can use VirtualBox to operate Linux in a virtual machine on the existing system. Running a Linux distribution as a virtual machine within VirtualBox in your Windows or Mac OS X environment is the same as running it in a Linux host environment, as mentioned in this chapter.

4.  Click on the specific link that corresponds to your Linux distribution and version.

    - Match the delivery version to the operating system you are using. If a VirtualBox version for your particular version is not yet available, grab the most recent version available. Chances are there that it'll still work.

5.  When the download begins, save the package to your computer's hard drive.

    - The installation procedure is lengthy and prone to failure. It is a safe idea to download the whole kit to your hard drive and install it from there.

6. Open your file manager and locate the VirtualBox installation package file. Double-click the package file.

   - To remove and install the Deb package in Ubuntu, you must first install a Package Manager application. The openSUSE Dolphin file manager knows what to do automatically.

   - VirtualBox requires the kernel header files to create modules that plug into the kernel. Before installing VirtualBox, you will probably need to install these packages first. Look up the package that installs the kernel header files in your Linux distribution's documentation. For openSUSE, it is kernel-default-devel.

7. Enter the administrative password when the package manager asks for it.

8. You might have a new VirtualBox entry added to your desktop menu system. In the KDE menu, openSUSE places the menu entry under the Applications System section.

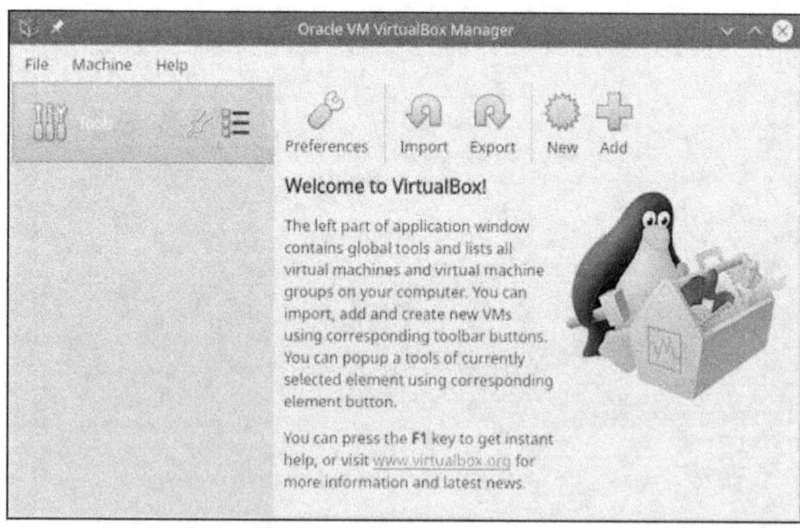

9.  You can build virtual machines once you have gotten to the main window!

## 3.2 Installing Linux on Physical Hardware

There are several steps to installing any Linux distribution, and we will walk you through them briefly and without going into too much detail. Then you can install what you want by following the comprehensive instructions for each delivery.

Before installing any Linux distributions, you will need a lot of knowledge about your computer's hardware. Before beginning the installation of Debian, gather information about your PC and its peripheral components.

Most Linux installation programs, fortunately, will detect and operate with the majority of PC peripherals.

Nonetheless, knowing your PC's hardware is a good idea so you can troubleshoot if anything goes wrong during the installation.

### Following The Important Steps:

The first move is to burn the media used for distribution. Any device with a burner capable of burning DVDs or CDs will do so. (A DVD burner must burn a DVD; however, a DVD burner can burn both CDs and DVDs.) If you already have a Windows PC with a CD/DVD burner, you can usually burn the CDs using that system.

Ensure that your computer can boot from the drive containing the media. While most new PCs can boot directly from a DVD/CD drive, some may need your assistance. Typically, the PC is programmed to boot from the hard drive before the DVD/CD drive, and changing the order of boot devices requires going into Setup.

To make a PC boot from a DVD drive, go into Setup when the computer turns on. The exact steps for entering Setup and selecting a boot device differ by PC, but they usually include pressing a key, such as F2. A brief message appears when the computer turns on, instructing you on which key to press to enter Setup.

You may designate the DVD drive as the boot system while in Setup. Insert the DVD or CD into the DVD drive and restart your computer after being set up to boot from the DVD drive.

The third move is to boot your PC from the Live CD or DVD to try a Live CD delivery. Otherwise, the third move is to make space on your PC's hard drive for Linux. This move can be challenging or straightforward if you are using Microsoft Windows, depending on whether you want to replace Windows with Linux or retain Windows and a Linux distribution.

Know that your current operating system uses the entire hard drive to install Linux without deleting (or disturbing) Windows. You will need to partition (divide) the hard drive so Windows can live on one side and Linux on the other. Partitioning can be a frightening move because you risk wiping out anything on the hard drive. Always create a backup of your essential data before making any significant changes.

You can use a partitioning tool to build a partition on your hard drive that the Linux installation program will use. If your computer is running the latest Windows 10 or an older version of Windows, consider purchasing a commercial hard drive partitioning software. But you can use a GUI (graphical user interface) tool named QTParted, which comes with Knoppix and many other distributions, to repartition your PC's hard drive.

Notice that some Linux distribution installers, such as openSUSE, will automatically build Linux partitions by shrinking a Windows partition. There, you will not need to shrink the Windows partition on your hard drive with a method like QTParted.

After you have set aside a partition on your hard drive for Linux, you can boot your computer from the DVD that came with your chosen distribution and begin the Linux installation. Several measures are involved in the installation, and they differ from one delivery to the next. It should be easy sailing now that you have made it this far. You will be finished in an hour or two if you just go through the installation screens. Most installers, such as the openSUSE interface, have a graphical user interface that walks you through each stage.

Partitioning the hard drive again is a crucial move during installation, but this time you simply use the extra partition you built.

Pick the software packages to install after completing a few Setup steps, such as setting up the network and time zone and letting the installer finish the remaining installation chores.

Some distributions simplify the process by eliminating the software selection stage and installing a default collection of software packages. Restart the PC after completing the installation. Until the automatic configuration runs, you will need to reboot.

When you first boot up Linux, you can complete some additional configuration measures and install additional software packages.

### Analyzing Your System's Hardware:

If you are worried that your PC cannot run Linux, here are some of the most critical components to remember before you begin the Linux installation:

**DVD drive:** Your computer must have a DVD drive (either a DVD-ROM or a DVD burner) and be able to boot from it.

It makes no difference what model you use. What matters is the way the DVD drive is connected to the computer. DVD drives attach to the hard drive controller on most new PCs (IDE, Integrated Drive Electronics, or ATA, for AT Attachment). An external DVD drive would probably attach to the USB port. In Linux, any IDE/ATA or USB DVD drive will function.

**Hard drives:** Linux accepts every IDE disc drive. SCSI (Small Computer System Interface) is another hard drive controller that Linux supports. You will need about 5GB of hard drive space to install and play with Linux comfortably. You need no hard drive space to check out the Live CD versions of Linux.

**Keyboard:** With Linux and the X Window System, any keyboard will function.

**Monitor:** The monitor is not essential, except that it must display the video card's screen resolutions. The pixels (horizontally and vertically) determine the screen resolution (such as 1024 x 768). The installer detects many modern monitors. If the installer does not detect your monitor, you can choose a generic monitor model with a specific resolution (such as 1024 x 768). You can also identify a monitor by its make and model, which can be found on the monitor's back.

**Mouse:** The installation software can detect the mouse. With Linux and the X Window System, any mouse (PS/2 or USB) will function.

**Network card:** While network cards are not standard on all PCs, they are becoming increasingly uncommon. Whether or not your PC has a Wi-Fi or wired network card, the installer should be able to identify and use it. If you have issues, try to locate the network card's make and model so you can look up whether Linux supports that card online.

**Processor:** As long as the processor speed is over 700 MHz (megahertz) or GHz (gigahertz), it doesn't matter. Most processors produced in the last few years have speeds far above that. The quicker, the better, as a general rule. Other Intel-compatible processors, such as AMD and VIA processors, will run Linux.

**RAM:** RAM refers to the memory available to your computer. The more RAM, like processing speed, the better. To install both Linux and the X Window System, you will need at least 512MB of RAM. Some distributions have a higher minimum memory requirement, and you will need even more to run a GUI desktop comfortably.

**SCSI controller:** SCSI controllers link disc drives and other peripherals to a PC in individual high-performance PCs and legacy workstations. If your PC has a SCSI controller, learn more about the controller's make and model.

**Sound card:** If your PC has a sound card and you want to use it with Linux, make sure the card is compatible. After successfully installing Linux, you can customize the sound card.

**Video card:** In text mode, Linux works with any video card (also known as monitor adapter), but if you want the graphical user interface, you will need a video card that supports the X Window System. The installer can detect a supported video card and correctly configure the X Window System. If the installer cannot detect your video card, knowing the make and model of the card is helpful.

**Printer:** Its make and model must identify every printer you plan to use in Linux.

Many Linux distributions, such as Debian GNU/Linux, will run on any hardware that supports the Linux kernel. To see if your PC's hardware is compatible with a specific distribution, go to the vendor's website and look at their hardware compatibility list.

<u>**Freeing Up Space for Your Linux Distribution:**</u>

Windows is installed on a single large partition on a standard Windows PC, taking up the entire hard drive. To make space for Linux, you will need to shrink the partition. The installation software uses the free space for the Linux partitions during the Linux installation.

There is no need to repartition your hard drive to try the Live CD distributions, such as Ubuntu. Simply boot your computer from the Live CD. You need not perform the repartitioning phase because the installers will shrink a Windows partition without destroying it. You must repartition your hard drive to install Fedora, Debian, or any other Linux distribution on it. You can use a commercial product to resize the disc partitions under Windows. You can boot a Linux distribution and then use GParted (the partition editor) to resize the Windows partitions. GParted can resize NTFS (NT File System) partitions used for all recent Windows versions.

The risk of losing all the data on the hard drive when you resize the disc partition still exists. Make a backup of your hard drive before using a disc partitioning tool to resize partitions.

Ensure you can recover your files from the backup after you have made your backup before doing something about the partitions.

Follow these steps to shrink the Windows partition after Ubuntu boots, and the GUI desktop appears:

1.  From the Ubuntu desktop, choose System Administration GParted.

    - The GParted window opens, and the tool lists the drives it discovers on your computer. The first hard drive is identified by the device name /dev/sda; the second is identified by the device name /dev/sdb, and so on.

2.  From the list of devices on the right side of the GParted window, select the hard drive.

3.  Pick the partition you want to resize from the list of partitions.

    - Usually, the largest partition is this one. The partition class for Windows 10, Windows 8, and other recent versions are NTFS, as shown by the Type column in the partitions list. Two partitions may be present in a typical new PC: a small fat16 partition and a sizeable NTFS partition.

4. Select GParted Resize/Move from the drop-down menu.

   - The dialogue box for resizing partitions appears.

5. Change the partition's size and then press Resize/Move.

   - After the partition, you can select a size that leaves you with at least 4GB of free space. The Free Space After field in the dialogue box displays the size of the free space.

6. When you have specified the adjustments you want to make, click Apply to start the process.

7. Click Apply when the alert appears.

   - All pending operations have been completed, the partition has been updated, and you now have free space after the Windows partition has been removed.

   - After you have freed up the space for Linux, you can install your preferred Linux distribution.

**<u>Try Out A Live CD Before Installing:</u>**

Try a Live CD or bootable USB version before installing something. You may typically perform a few additional preinstallation chores besides having a feel for a Linux desktop.

For example, to start Ubuntu, boot your computer from the Live CD. A menu appears, allowing you to choose from several choices to control the boot phase or check your device to see whether it meets hardware specifications. You can choose the default choice for booting Ubuntu (which will be done automatically if you do not make a selection before the menu expires in 30 seconds).

After a few minutes, the GNOME GUI desktop, which Ubuntu uses, appears, and you can explore Ubuntu. When you open the Examples folder, you will see several things Ubuntu can do. You may also use System Administration GParted to change the hard drive's configuration.

When done with Ubuntu, select System Quit, delete the DVD, and click Enter when Ubuntu has shut down. If you plan to install Ubuntu, start the process by clicking the Install icon on the desktop.

## Installing Linux

Bootable USB distributions have been around for a while, but they've always had flaws that kept me from using them.    However, newer ones, such as Fedora Media Writer (https://github.com/MartinBriza/MediaWriter), have streamlined the development process to where most users can walk through it without assistance. The installation process is non-destructive, which means you can keep your existing files on the USB drive, and data persistence is easy.

We will show you how to make a bootable flash drive and use it in your environment in the rest of this chapter.

## Making A Bootable USB Flash Drive

While command-line methods in Linux can build a bootable flash drive, the most straightforward method is to use Windows.    (We realize that making a Linux boot medium from Windows might seem heretical, but most users interested in a Live USB implementation of Linux are Windows users.) To make a bootable flash drive, follow these steps:

1.  Get the bootable software you want to use.

2.  Run the software after installation.

3.  Pick the flash drive in the Target Device section.

    -  The flash drive could have a name like TravelDrive on it.

4.  Choose the source of the image (the ISO file).

    -  If your Internet connection is weak, you can use a single Live CD to pull the ISO file. Use the Download option to access an ISO file if you have a faster Internet connection.

5.  If asked, set persistent storage.

- The storage space allocated to the installation still available is known as persistent storage. We recommend a size of at least 300MB.

6. Press the Create Live USB button and wait for the process to finish.

- Expect a ten-minute wait for the process to end. On most hard drives, two directories are created: syslinux (less than 7MB and responsible for booting) and LiveOS (the size of which depends on your storage setting).

7. Exit the program and test the newly created bootable drive.

## Workstation Troubleshooting

We tried multiple flash drives and never had a problem with any of them as long as there was 1GB of free space after download. Smaller drives (2GB or less) are often factory-formatted with FAT (File Allocation Table), whereas larger drives are formatted with FAT32. Formatting had little effect on installation or usability, as far as we could tell.

Ensure that the workstation's settings enable it to boot from USB, which usually necessitates BIOS reconfiguration. To do so, take these steps:

1. Restart the computer and press the key that takes you to the BIOS settings.

2. This key is usually F12 or DEL, but it may also be F1 or F2.

3. Go to the Boot Menu and select the Boot USB Devices First choice (or something similar).

4. The flash drive may be concealed in the hard drive portion of the boot BIOS on some computers. Choose Boot Hard Drives, change the primary hard drive to the storage media, and then make sure the USB is the first option under Boot Device. Choose"Enable, go to the order of boot devices, and transfer the USB selection above the hard drive selection if the option to boot from USB is Enable/ Disable.

5. Exit the BIOS setup and save your changes.

The workstation will reboot at this stage, and if your USB drive is plugged in, Fedora should boot.

If the single-line entry Boot Error appears and nothing else occurs, follow the manufacturer's instructions to update the device BIOS.

### Working with The Latest Drive Regularly

The Fedora environment loads much faster than the Live CD environment when your machine boots. The new files generated on the USB drive are visible, and other devices can be accessed commonly. The"Install to Hard Drive" icon remains on the screen, allowing you to make a fast and permanent switch to Fedora if you so desire.

While getting an Internet connection is unnecessary to use the operating system, we highly advise it because most users would want to download additional programs to test the operating system's functionality further.

Congratulations on your achievement! You can now begin to use Linux.

## 3.3 Installing Linux on Virtual Machines on Windows 10

You must complete some additional virtual machine setup before you can access your virtual world. Since the New Virtual Machine Wizard creates a generic world, you will want to customize it first. This segment explains how to configure the virtual machine and how to install your operating system.

### Adjusting The Settings

VirtualBox collects configuration options for each virtual machine you build. VirtualBox emulates what is defined in these configuration settings in the virtual machine.

Pick the virtual machine entry on the left-hand side and press the"Settings" icon in the toolbar to access the configuration settings. The Settings dialogue box appears.

On the left-hand side of the Settings dialogue box, ten configuration categories are shown by icons with text:

**General**: General Setting defines the virtual machine's name and operating system type. You will enable the clipboard on the Advanced tab to copy and paste text, files, and directories between the host and guest systems.

**System**: Controls the virtual machine's CPU and memory allocation.

**Display**: This component manages the virtual machine's video memory and virtual displays.

**Storage**: Controls access to virtual hard drives and DVD drive emulation. The virtual hard drive you have built should be mentioned here, but you can add more if necessary. You can also give the virtual machine access to the host system's DVD drive from here. Another cool feature of VirtualBox is installing an ISO image file on the guest device directly. You can now install Linux distributions directly from ISO image files instead of burning them to DVD.

Ensure you mount the DVD drive in the DVD section if you will install the virtual machine operating system from a DVD. Unfortunately, that option is not available by design.

**Audio**: Controls access to the host system's sound card. You can choose the ALSA driver for Linux hosts to enable the virtual server to transmit sound to the host Linux sound system.

**Network**: The virtual machine will link to the host system's network, where you configure that function. Between the virtual machine and the host device, the default NAT option generates an internal network. This creates a barrier between the virtual machine and the rest of the network, preventing other devices from accessing the virtual machine. This is useful if you are testing an operating system and want to keep it beside the rest of your network. Pick the Bridged network option instead if you want the virtual machine to have complete access to your local network.     The virtual server's network interface can then link to the network on the host server.

**Serial Ports**: If open, control access to the host system's serial communication ports.

**USB**: Make a list of the USB devices on the host system you want to use on the guest system.

**Shared Folders**: This feature allows you to build a folder accessible from both the host system and the virtual machine. This creates a simple file transfer pipeline between the two environments.

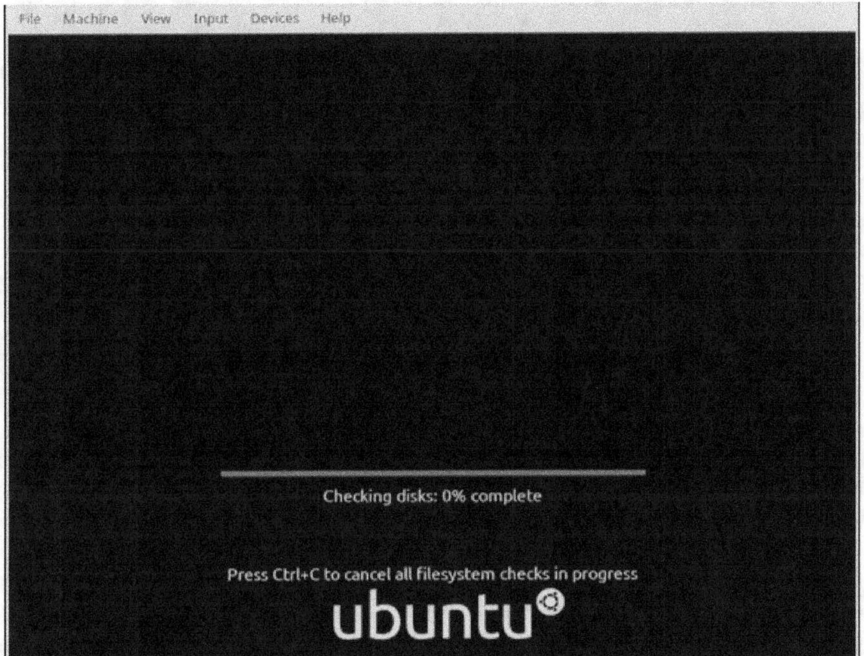


**User Interface**: Select which menu bar features you want to be enabled for virtual machine power.

After you have customized your settings, click "**OK**" to save them and return to the VirtualBox main window. You are all set to install some apps now!

### Installing the OS

You are ready to go now that the virtual machine has been customized for your new operating system. However, before you begin, double-check that you have the DVD or USB drive required for the installation. After you have got that, you can install it by following these steps:

1. Insert the operating system installation DVD into the host system's CD/DVD player, or use the virtual machine's DVD drive to access the ISO image file. If your desktop opens a file manager program by default, you can close it before continuing. It is normal for the disc to be installed on the device and appear as a desktop icon. From the left-hand list, choose the virtual machine on which you want to install the operating system.

2. Select the Start icon from the toolbar. This switches on the virtual machine as if you had switched on the hardware's power switch. The console emulation window in VirtualBox appears. This window contains all that would usually show on display.

3. When the virtual machine is accessing hardware on the device, icons at the bottom of the window indicate this. The icons are:

   - The hard disc drive

   - The DVD player

   - Audio input and output

   - The network link

   - The USB link

   - The folder exchanged

   - Memory for video

   - Making a recording

   - The state of the CPU

   A mouse icon, a key icon, and the word Right Ctrl can all be found in the browser's bottom-right corner. When you start the virtual machine, VirtualBox takes control of the host system's keyboard and mouse and gives it to the virtual machine. Press the Control (Ctrl) key on the right side of the keyboard to return control to the host device (for example, to run another program simultaneously). Place the mouse anywhere within the console emulation window and press the right Ctrl key to regain control of the virtual machine.

4. Complete the installation of the operating system you are using.

5. The DVD or ISO file is used to start the virtual machine (refer to the General section of the Settings dialogue box). Simply observe the operating system's usual installation procedure. The operating system detects the emulated hardware you installed in the virtual machine

6. When the installation is over, reboot the virtual machine.

7. The majority of Operating Systems (OS) comes with a built-in reboot feature. If this occurs, the VirtualBox console emulation window detects the reboot and remains open, allowing you to observe the reboot.

The result is a functional operating system that runs inside your virtual machine.

## 3.4 Installing Linux On Virtual Machines On MacOS

Your Mac has a lot of power, a long battery life, and a lot of durability. A Mac's hardware is hard to beat, making it a powerful machine for operating Linux.

Linux gives new life to outdated Macs that can no longer get macOS updates. Rather than having your old MacBook Pro become an unnecessary paperweight, upgrade to the new version of Linux and run the system for years.

Both Linux and macOS are enabled on your Mac when you use a dual boot system. When your computer is booting up, hold the option to pick on what operating system to utilize. The essential differentiator between a virtual machine and a dual-boot system is that dual-booting allows you to use only one operating system simultaneously, but it provides better performance.

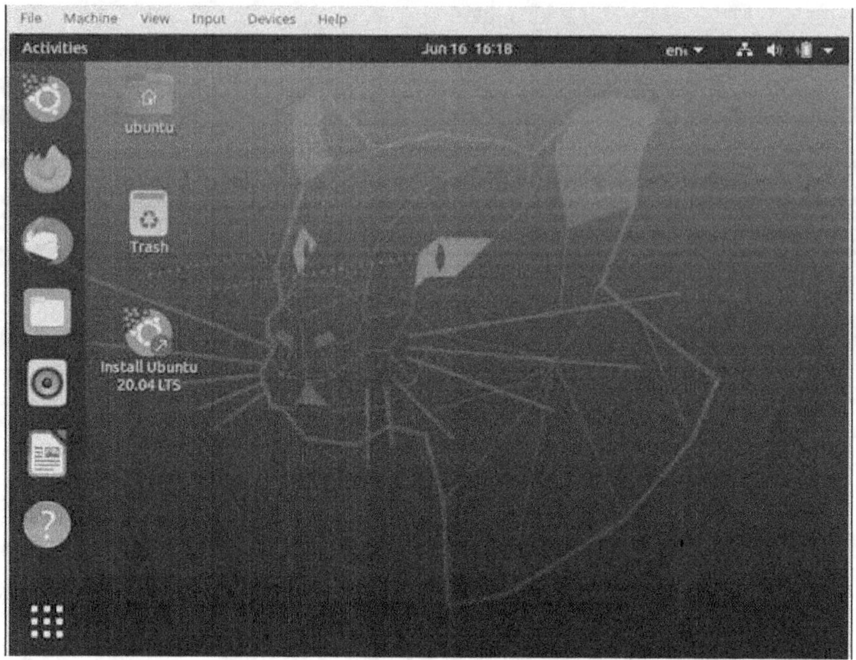



If you do not intend to use macOS anyway, you might like to replace it with Linux. That way, the machine files do not eat up any of your storage.

However, if you reconsider, restoring macOS is complicated and time-consuming. As Linux writes over the macOS Recovery partition, this is true. If you are sure that you do not want to use the dual-booting option and go for the Virtual Machine setup, skip the Partition phase and proceed to the installation process.

- A flash drive with at least 2GB of storage is needed to run Linux on your Mac. To mount Ubuntu on the flash drive, you will need to erase it first. Please ensure you have backed up any essential data first.

- Link your Mac to the internet with an Ethernet adapter. This is critical because, without third-party drivers, your Wi-Fi can not work in Ubuntu. In the same way, iMac users can get a USB keyboard or mouse if Bluetooth fails.

- To have a dual boot, try to ensure you have enough available space on your hard drive.

- Verify that you have at minimum 25GB of free space by going to the Apple menu > About This Mac > Storage.

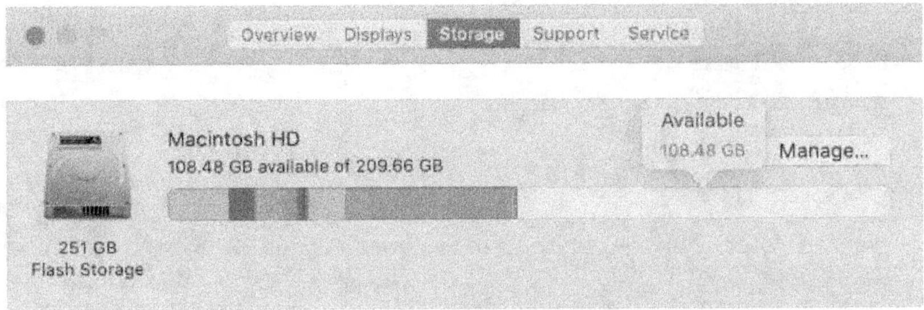


- Last but not least, create a backup of your Mac. By deploying Linux in a dual boot partition, you should not lose any data. If something goes wrong, you will need to wipe your Mac clean to restore it.

- Instead of building a dual-boot setup, use Carbon Copy Cloner for backing up your macOS Recovery partition to replace macOS with Linux. This makes reverting to macOS a lot simpler.

### Booting from USB Installer:

Restart your Mac while keeping the option and insert the USB flash drive into the computer directly. Once the boot loader shows, pick Boot EFI with the arrow keys and press"Enter."

The Ubuntu desktop appears after the Ubuntu loading screen. Take advantage of this opportunity to try Ubuntu on your Mac. Remember that it could be slow because it is operating from a USB flash drive. Using an Ethernet cable to link to the internet since Ubuntu can't use the Mac's Wi-Fi by design.

### Installing Linux on Mac

Double-click the "Install Ubuntu" icon on the desktop when set. To select your keyboard layout and languages, execute the on-screen prompts. Select a Normal installation and the Install third-party software option. Installing this app, which allows you to use Wi-Fi and Bluetooth, requires connecting your Mac to the internet with an Ethernet cable. Then press the Continue button. Keep the partitions mounted if asked.

### Setting Up the Boot Manager

Your Mac's default boot manager does not always operate for Ubuntu. This means you must deploy a third-party boot manager anyway, which will allow you to easily switch between macOS and Linux when your computer boots up.

The next move is to install rEFInd. You must briefly deactivate System Integrity Protection to enable rEFInd. Allow it again afterward because this is an essential security function for macOS

To set up the rEFInd boot manager, follow these steps:

- Launch Terminal from the Utility folder in Applications with SIP disabled.

- In a different window, open Finder and switch to the rEFInd link.

- Click Enter after dragging the rEFInd-install package into your Terminal window.

- Enter your user account when asked, then click "Enter" again.

- Remember to re-enable SIP after the installation is complete.

- Dropping the rEFInd-install file into a Terminal window and entering the code.

- The rEFInd selection should automatically appear the next instant you reboot your Mac. Keep Option when booting up to launch your boot manager if it does not.

# CHAPTER 4
# LINUX SHELL

You will need to connect with the machine and tell it what you want it to do. One way to communicate with a machine in Linux is via a program called the shell. A shell is not a graphical interface. It is the set of commands and syntax to complete your tasks.

By graphical desktop norms, the shell environment is very bland and boring. When you first launch the shell, you will see a short prompt, such as a $, followed by a blinking cursor waiting for you to type something.

## 4.1 What is Shell?

A command shell, also known as a command interpreter, is a program that sends the commands to the operating system and application programs and receiving their responses. It is comparable to command.com in MS-DOS or cmd.exe in Windows in terms of functions, but the Linux shell is much more functional. Scripts are small programs written in the command shell language that perform sequential operations with files and their data.

It is difficult to be a successful Linux professional without understanding how to use the command line.

The command line is a shell prompt that shows whether the device is ready to accept a user command. This is called a user-system dialogue. The user receives a response from the system for each command entered:

1. A new invitation, indicating that the command has been executed and that you will proceed to the next step.

2. An error message is a statement from the system to the user about events in the system.

Working with the command line can seem inconvenient to users used to working with systems with a graphical interface. This form of GUI has always been basic in Linux and thus well developed. There are several ways to save effort, and keystrokes when performing the most common behavior in the Linux command shells:

- Long command or file names are automatically added

- Scanning for and re-executing an executed command

- File name list substitutions based on a standard and much more

When you need to conduct identical operations on several items, the command line's advantages become apparent. In a graphical interface system, you will need as many input devices as there are objects. On the command line, one command will suffice.

This chapter will go over the essential resources you can use to solve any user task using the command line. It ranges from basic file and directory operations like copying, renaming, and searching to more complicated tasks involving massive related operations like those found in user applications, dealing with large data arrays or text, and in system administration.

## 4.2 Gaining Access to Shell

The bash shell is the default shell in Linux. The Bourne shell, also known as sh, is a UNIX shell used in this work environment. The Bourne again shell is what the word bash refers to. Most Linux distributions have the bash shell.

A terminal program on your GUI desktop can launch a bash session. The terminal program you use is determined by your desktop:

- The default terminal in the GNOME 3 desktop is Terminal. Pick the Terminal icon from the program launcher, or type Terminal into the Search text box if you do not see it.

- The default terminal in the KDE Plasma desktop is Konsole. To open it, go to the K menu and choose Applications System Konsole.

The shell command line prompt is the prompt in the window. Your commands are typed in there.

Additional cool features in both Terminal and Konsole include cutting and pasting text and changing the color of the text and context. You can also use green text on a black screen, much like the computer terminals in old movies from the 1970s.

## 4.3 Types of Shell

A command shell, also known as a command interpreter, is a program that sends the commands to the operating system and application programs and receiving their responses. It compares to command.com in MS-DOS or cmd.exe in Windows in terms of tasks, but the Linux shell is incomparably more affluent in terms of functionality. Scripts are small programs written in the command shell language that perform sequential operations with files and their data.

You can see a command line prompt – a line ending in $ – after you have registered in the system by entering a username and password. This symbol will represent the command line. You could get to the command line on any virtual text console if a graphical user interface were configured to start at the system boot during the installation. You can do this by pressing Ctrl-Alt-F1 - Ctrl-Alt-F6 or by using a terminal emulator program like xterm.

The shells listed below are available. Depending on the distributor, they can differ:

**Bash**

The most famous Linux shell. It can connect to the names of commands and files, maintains a command history, and allows you to edit them.

**pdkdh**

On UNIX shell systems, the Korn shell clone is well-known.

**sash**

This shell is unique because it does not depend on any shared libraries and contains simpler versions of some of the most commonly used utilities, such as al, dd, and gzip. The sash comes in handy when recovering from machine crashes or updating the versions of the most critical shared libraries.

**tcsh**

Upgraded version of C shell.

**zsh**

This is the most recent shell on the list. It includes advanced features such as command argument autocompletion and a slew of other features that make working with the shell much more convenient and practical. However, since all zsh extensions are disabled by default, you must read the documentation and allow the features you need before using this command shell.

Bash Bourne Again Shell is the shell by default. Use the command echo $ SHELL to see which shell you are using.

Shells vary not only in terms of functionality but also in terms of command syntax. If you are a new user, we suggest that you start with bash. Additional examples explain this area's work.

**Bash shell**

The command line in bash consists of the command's name followed by keys (options), which alter the command's actions. Keys usually start with the character–or–and consist of only one letter. After the command, arguments (parameters)–the names of the objects on which the command must be executed–can be added (often the names of files and directories).

After pressing the Enter key to finish entering a command, the command is moved to the execution shell. There may appear messages about the command execution or errors resulting from the command execution on the user's Terminal. The appearance of the following command line prompt (ending with the $ character) means that the command has been completed, and you can enter the next one.

In bash, many techniques make typing and editing the command line simpler. You may, for example, use the keyboard to:

| **CTRL-A** |
| --- |
| Return to the start of the line. By pressing the Home key, you can achieve the same result. |
| |
| **CTRL-U** |
| This command should remove the present line; |
| |
| **CTRL-C** |
| Abort the current command's execution. |

You may use the symbol to enter several commands in a single line. Bash keeps track of all commands performed, making it simple to go back and repeat or edit one of them. Pick the desired command from the history: the up key displays the previous command, the down key displays the down command, and this key displays the next command.

To find a particular command among those that have been executed without going through the entire story, press Ctrl-R and enter a keyword used in the command you are searching for.

The commands documented in history are numbered—type ":" to run a particular command.

**! command number**

If you type "!!", the last command you typed will be executed.

On Linux, software and command names can be excessively long. Fortunately, bash will finish the names for you. You may complete the name of a command, program, or directory by pressing the Tab key.

Let's say you want to use the bunzip2 decompression program as an example. To do so, type:

**$ bu**

Then click the Tab key. If nothing happens, there are a few other options for completing the command. By pressing the Tab key once more, you will get a list of names that begin with the letter bu. The framework, for example, contains these programs: buildhash, builtin, and bunzip2:

**$ bu**

buildhash builtin bunzip2

**$ bu**

Click Tab after typing n> (bunzip is the only name with the letter n as the third letter). The shell will complete the remaining part of the name for you, and all you have to do now is to press"Enter" to execute the command.

Bash searches directories specified in the PATH system variable for programs invoked from the command line.

By default, the directory, denoted by. /, is not included in this directory listing (dot slash). You must use the command. /prog to run the program from the directory.

## 4.4 Shell Scripting

Frequently, the information in your shell prompt is useful. If you are logged in as rich on Ubuntu's system testbox, for example, your prompt will look like this:

**rich@testbox:~$**

You are in the"Home"folder, as indicated by the tilde character (~). The dollar sign means the bash shell is ready for me to type a command.

Before you go through some of the shell's features, We want to tell you about another way to start a shell session. You may not use it often, but it may come in handy at some stage. Foremost, keep in mind that your shell prompt is contained inside a window on your GUI desktop. Assume you want your whole computer to be text-only.

As Linux distribution boots, it launches one or more virtual terminals. Each virtual terminal functions as a separate physical terminal with its shell. To move to a different virtual terminal, press Ctrl+Alt+F#, where # is a virtual terminal number from 1 to 8, and # is a virtual terminal number from 1 to 8. The trick is that various Linux distributions use different virtual terminals for their default graphical shell.

To switch between virtual terminals, press Ctrl+Alt on your keyboard. If your familiar graphical desktop vanishes, do not panic. It is already running in the background, and you can pick up right where you left off in a matter of seconds. Examine the screen configuration once you have found a text-based virtual terminal.

You have most likely seen something similar to this:

*testbox login:*

Fill in the blanks with your username and password when prompted. A message with your last login date appears, followed by the bash prompt:

*rich@testbox:~$*

Note how close this prompt is to the open window you left on the GUI desktop. Both prompts indicate that you are in a bash session, while they are both the product of using the bash shell, they are separate and distinct instances of the same program. The world you are operating in here is separate from the bash environment you are already using in the GUI terminal window.

Are you curious where your graphical user interface (GUI) desktop has vanished to? Jumping around between the virtual terminals can help to relax the nerves. Just a few virtual terminals provide a graphical desktop environment, while the majority use a text-based login. Turn to the one where your original desktop session was located. Your computer can flash for a second or two before returning you to your graphical desktop. Isn't it cool?

What's more, guess what? You never signed out of the bash session you left open on the other virtual Terminal. Press Ctrl+Alt plus the feature key for that virtual terminal session to return to it. Voilà! — everything is just as you left it. Turn between VTs and skip back and forth a few times (F1 through F8). What a joy! This virtual terminal thing is fantastic.

Your GUI session is locked when you use the Lock Screen function for your desktop. Ctrl+Alt may switch to a virtual terminal by anyone. So, before you leave your machine, log out of your virtual terminals.

When you have had your fill of this little trick, exit (literally, type exit) to log out of any VTs you have opened and click the Ctrl+Alt shortcut to return to your graphical desktop and bash prompt. After that, you will see what all the fuss is about with this shell gadget.

## 4.5 Basic Command Line Editing

Since a shell interprets what you write, it is crucial to understand how the shell interprets the text you enter. This is the general format of all shell commands:

command option1 option2 ... optionN

A command line is a term for a single line of commands. You enter a command accompanied by one or more optional parameters on a command line (or arguments). These command-line options (or arguments) allow you to decide what the command should do.

To separate the command from the options and separate options from one another, use a space or a tab. You must place a choice that includes embedded spaces inside quotation marks to use it. Enter the grep command to scan for two words of text in the password file, for example. (grep is a command that searches for text in files in a cryptic manner).

**grep "WWW daemon" /etc/passwd**

The output of grep on the line containing those words looks like this. (What you see on your screen can not be the same as what we show.

**wwwrun:x:30:8:WWW daemon apache:/var/lib/wwwrun:/bin/false**

If you built a user account with your name, use the grep command with your name as an argument, but remember to quote the name if it contains spaces.

As you understand the command line, you can discover some keyboard shortcuts to make your life easier. In this segment, we will show you how to use some of the bash shell's features to make your command-line experience as fun as possible.

Command-line completion, editing, and using the background of entered commands are among these functions.

## You can ask Linux to finish a command or filename for you.

Given you type much more on the command line in Linux than you would in a GUI environment, a feature that allows you to use typing shortcuts wherever possible is useful. The shell's Command completion feature completes filename and system commands.

Since the Linux file system can deal with nearly infinite filename sizes, many filenames can become enormous. It's time-consuming to type these long filenames. Thankfully, command completion makes typing a command or a long filename a breeze.

Use command completion for one of two things: entering a command or finishing a filename.

## Performing a command

Consider the following scenario: you want to type a command, but all you know is that it starts with the letters up and is expected to return the time since the machine was rebooted. At the command prompt, type up and then press Tab:

rich@testbox:~$ up[TAB]

## One of these scenarios occurs:

- If the search path (directory locations for searching for programs; type echo $PATH to discover what yours is) includes only one matching command, the command line is completed with that command, and the machine waits for you to press Enter to execute it.

- A beep implies that more than one command begins with the letter up. Press Tab a second time, and the options will appear.

Locate the command on the list and type it until the first letters are distinct, at which point you can complete the command by pressing the Tab key. There is no match if nothing is displayed after pressing Tab twice.

### Completing a File Name:

Do not type the first few characters and then press Tab to get command-line completion. If you are typing a filename on the command line, you have to type the first few characters and then press Tab. The shell typically scans the current working directory for filenames that fits what you have typed and then completes the command line filename. If more than one file contains the letters you type, you will hear a beep and need to press Tab again to see a list of options, just as with the command-completion function.

It takes some getting used to, but once you have mastered the Tab key and the shell command-line completion function, you will wonder how you managed without it.

### Browsing your command history

It is sweet of the shell to remember what you have done. The shell's ability to keep track of commands helps you to easily return to those obscenely long commands you pecked at a long time ago — even days ago! For example, suppose you located and removed all of your system's core dump files (core dump files are huge files containing debugging data that only an expert programmer or your machine would understand). The command was something along these lines:

find / -name core -exec rm {} \;

To re-run the command, retrieve it from your shell history and rerun it. The easiest way is to type.

Find and press"Enter"(if you are repeating the exact version of the command you used last time, which is the find command).  This instructs your system to search your history for the last instance of find in the list and rerun it.

If you have run the find command more than once and want to make sure you are re-running the correct version, you will need to look at your command history. By pressing the up-arrow key repeatedly before reaching the command you want to re-execute, you can do so line by line. Press the Enter key to rerun the command.

When you enter the history command at the prompt, it displays your last 20 commands (by default), if you are curious about what they were.

# CHAPTER 5

# LINUX COMMANDS

The keyboard dance that Linux experts usually perform is also awe-inspiring to computer newbies. These keyboard musicians know technological advancements such as the mouse and graphical interface, but they prefer the home keys and feel they can operate faster. It takes time to achieve this level of expertise, but every expert was once a novice, and with enough practice, every novice can become an expert.

According to what they can do for you, the command line commands have been organized into categories in this chapter.

## 5.1 System Control Commands

These commands provide information and control for the entire system. Regular users can run many commands that collect system information. However, commands that actively alter the system's configuration must be run when logged in as root — or have used the Su command to become the super user temporarily.

<u>Administrative Commands:</u>

| | |
|---|---|
| **Passwd** | Change a particular user's password. Any user can use this command to change their password. |
| **Su** | Switch to another user account without having to log out of the first one.<br>The ideal way to use this command is su — so your filesystem path and other information are loaded. |

## Kernel Support Commands:

You will likely need to add kernel support for a new system occasionally (software or hardware). If this situation happens, you have a few options:

The kernel can be rebuilt, or a loadable kernel module can be mounted. While rebuilding a kernel does not necessitate a nuclear science Ph.D., it is a time-consuming annoyance best avoided.

The table's commands allow you to add kernel support while the system is running, rather than having to rebuild it from the ground up.

| | |
|---|---|
| **Lsmod** | Lists the modules your kernel has loaded. |
| **depmod** | Regenerates your module dependencies. |
| **Insmod** | Loads a module by hand. |
| **Rmmod** | Unloads a module by hand. |
| **modprobe** | Loads a module along with its dependencies and settings. |

## Process Commands:

Processes are required for the majority of your system's activity. Many processes (programs) are running in the background even though the machine appears idle.

These commands, which are listed in the table, allow you to look under the hood to ensure that anything that needs to run is running and that you are not overheating or overburdening resources.

| | |
|---|---|
| **Crontab** | Sets up commands to execute at regular intervals. |
| **Kill** | Stops a process by its number. Often used as kill -9 for an abrupt stop for something that won't stop. |
| **Killall** | Stops a process by its name rather than the number. |

| | |
|---|---|
| **Nice** | Assigns a CPU utility priority to a process. |
| **Pidof** | Gets a program's or process's ID number. |
| **Ps** | Gets a lot of processes' ID numbers, usually used as ps aux. |
| **Pstree** | Shows the relationships between programs. |
| **Renice** | Changes a program's CPU use priority. |
| **Top** | Shows resource use. |

## Network Commands:

Even if it is just your small home network, most Linux systems are now connected to the internet. The graphical Network Manager tool helps you to customize your network settings in one location. Linux also includes a range of command-line tools for managing and fine-tuning the network settings. The table lists some of the more useful network-related commands.

| | |
|---|---|
| **Ethtool** | Displays Ethernet settings for a network interface. |
| **Ifconfig** | Displays or sets the IP address and netmask for a network interface. |
| **Ip** | Display or sets the IP address, netmask, and router for a network interface. |
| **Iw** | Displays or sets the wireless settings for a wireless network interface. |
| **iwconfig** | Displays or sets the SSID, IP address, and netmask for a wireless network interface. |
| **Nmcli** | Opens the Network Manager command-line interface. |
| **Nmtui** | Opens the Network Manager menu-based command-line tool. |
| **Route** | Displays or sets the default router information. |

## 5.2 Function Commands

Since every command has a distinct role, categorizing these tools into groups based on their roles is easy. If you know what process you need to run but are not sure which command will do the job, start your search here. You can go deeper by referring to man pages and other support material (online sites and reference books)

At a command prompt, type man command to get to a man tab. Man ls, for example, displays the file listing command's support information.

### Shell Help Commands:

When looking for support with a command, you have access to an exciting set of shell commands, as shown in the table.

Seeking knowledge about a command's command-prompt choices is a never-ending search. For quickly finding this detailed material, the man page system provides helpful guides at your fingertips.

| | |
|---|---|
| **Apropos** | Looks for commands containing a keyword in their man page descriptions. |
| **Info** | One way of finding helpful information. |
| **Man** | The standard way of getting help in Linux and UNIX. |
| **Whatis** | Gets a one-line description of a command. |

### Bash Commands:

When you try to look up the support details for any commands in the man pages, they do not seem to exist, and the commands do not appear as files on your system.

When you type commands at the prompt, remember that you are working with a shell program. (In my case, the default Linux shell is bash.) The shell collects commands you can use to communicate with it, mentioned in the following table.

| Alias | Creates or lists command shortcuts. |
|---|---|
| Unalias | Removes command shortcuts. |
| Env | Lists your currently running environment variables and their settings. |
| History | Lists of the last 1,000 commands you have typed. |
| Export | Whenever you are told to set an environment variable, create the variable and then use this command so that the variable will appropriately be remembered. |

When you view the man page entry for these commands, you get the BASH BUILTINS loads to support instead. To search this manual, open the man search GUI by pressing the forward-slash (/) key, then typing the name of the command you want to look up. To begin the quest, press"Enter."The interface comes to a halt the first time the word is encountered. Click the N key to go to the next occurrence of the term to try again.

For example, you may be reading the huge bash man page (type man bash to access this page), but you are only interested in prompts, which are the bits of text to the left of your cursor in a text window. A good example of a prompt is: rich@testbox:~$

To jump down to the first instance of this phrase, type /prompt, and press"Enter."If the text surrounding the word does not match what you are looking for, click the N key to move on to the next.

## Compressing and Comprising:

Although disc space is not as valuable as it once was, bandwidth and backup media are still in high demand. As shown in the table, this category offers various tools for compacting and organizing data for storage.

| bzip2 | Compresses files into .bz2 format. Used mostly for large sets of text files. |
|---|---|
| bunzip2 | Uncompresses .bz2 files. |

| gunzip | Uncompresses .gz files and .tgz files. |
|---|---|
| Unzip | Uncompresses files from .zip format. |
| Compress | Compresses files into .Z format. |
| Xz | Compresses and uncompresses files from .xz format. |
| Tar | Packages files together in a group. The standard way of using this command is tar xvf filename, such as tar xvf download.tar. |
| Gzip | Compresses files into .gz format. |
| Uncompress | Uncompresses files from .Z format. |
| Zip | Compresses files into .zip format. |

## 5.3 File System Commands

It is challenging to do something without navigating and working with the filesystem, regardless of which operating system you are using. These tools will assist you in locating your position.

### General File System Commands:

These commands, specified in the table, provide information or perform actions on the entire filesystem from development and tuning to repair and recovery. Some of these commands return info, while others give you surgical tools for serious filesystem hacking.

| e2label | Applies a filesystem label to an ext2 or ext3 partition. |
|---|---|
| badblocks | Searches a partition for bad blocks. |
| Eject | Ejects a CD or DVD. |
| e2fsck | Checks and repairs an ext2 or ext3 filesystem. |

| | |
|---|---|
| **Mkfs** | Creates a filesystem (format a partition). |
| **Fsck** | Can check and repair many types of filesystems. |
| **Mount** | Loads a partition into your filesystem. |
| **Umount** | Removes a partition from the filesystem. |
| **Sync** | Saves all information out of buffers onto disks. |
| **tune2fs** | Adjusts ext2 and ext3 filesystem parameters. |

## File Organization Commands:

As shown in the table, file organization commands provide tools for moving files and filesystem units around.

| | |
|---|---|
| **Cp** | Copies a file. |
| **Df** | Shows partitions and how much space they have. |
| **Ls** | Lists the contents of a directory or information about a file. |
| **Mkdir** | Creates a directory. |
| **Cd** | Changes directories. |
| **Du** | Shows how much disk is being used in the directory and below. |
| **Ln** | Creates a shortcut. |
| **Mv** | Moves or renames a file. |
| **Rmdir** | Deletes an empty directory. |
| **Pwd** | Shows the path for the directory you are in. |
| **Rm** | Deletes a file. |

## File Location Commands:

The commands mentioned in the following table, assist you in finding files in Linux's massive tree-structure filesystem.

| | |
|---|---|
| **Find** | Hard-core filesystem search tool. |
| **Locate** | Lighter-weight filesystem search tool. |
| **Which** | Tells you the path for the program run if you typed this command. |

## File Attributes Commands:

Files are similar to candy bars. The wrappers list the ingredients, size, and date of manufacture, which are descriptive of the tasty nugget inside. (Perhaps the wrapper is child-resistant) the wrapper information is stored in an inode in files.

Besides changing file inode information, these commands can also return data about the file's content, as shown in the table.

| | |
|---|---|
| **Chgrp** | Changes the group associated with a file. |
| **Stat** | Shows statistics about the file. |
| **Wc** | Shows how many words, lines, and so on are in this file. |
| **Chmod** | Changes a file's permissions. |
| **File** | Shows what type of file you are dealing with. |
| **Chown** | Changes who owns a file. |
| **Touch** | Creates an empty file of this name. |

<u>**File Viewer Commands:**</u>

Many a device user's favorite pastime is searching text files. These programs provide a wide range of functions for displaying the contents of readable text files of various sizes. Since these commands are just viewers, not editors, you can't harm the contents of a file with them, as with a full-screen editor.

| | |
|---|---|
| **Head** | Shows the initial ten lines of a file. |
| **More** | Shows the file a screen at a time, forward only. |
| **Less** | Shows the file a screen at a time, forward and backward. |
| **Tail** | Shows the last ten lines of a file. |
| **Cat** | Dumps the contents of the file to your screen. |

<u>**Processing File Commands:**</u>

These commands listed below help users process files in the filesystem.

| | |
|---|---|
| **Cat** | Displays a file in standard output (can concatenate several files into one big file). |
| **Diff** | Compares two text files and finds differences. |
| **Cut** | Extracts particular sections from each line of text in a file. |
| **Dd** | Copies blocks of data from one file to another (used to copy data from devices). |
| **Expand** | Converts all tabs to spaces. |
| **Fold** | Wraps each line of text to fit a specified width. |
| **File** | Displays the data in a file. |
| **Grep** | Searches for regular expressions in a text file. |

| Lpr | Prints files. |
|---|---|
| Less | Displays a text file one page at a time. (Go backward by pressing b.) |
| More | Displays a text file one page at a time. (Goes forward only). |
| Paste | Concatenates corresponding lines from several files. |
| Nl | Numbers all nonblank lines in a text file and prints the lines to standard output. |
| Patch | Updates a text file by using the differences between the original and revised copies of the file. |
| Sort | Sorts lines in a text file. |
| Sed | Copies a file to standard output while applying specified editing commands. |
| Split | Breaks up a file into several smaller files with specified sizes. |
| Tac | Reverses a file (last line first and so on). |
| Zcat | Displays a compressed file (after decompressing). |
| Tail | Displays the last few lines of a file. |
| Tr | Substitutes one group of characters for another throughout a file. |
| Uniq | Eliminates duplicate lines from a text file. |
| zmore | Displays a compressed file, one page at a time. |
| Wc | Counts the lines, words, and characters in a text file. |
| Zless | Displays a compressed file, one page at a time. (Go backward by pressing b.) |

## 5.4 Becoming Superuser (Root)

You must become root to do something that demands high privilege, such as administering your scheme. Typically, you log in as daily use with your usual username and password. When you need superuser rights, however, run the following command to become root: su -

Su, followed by a space, and the minus sign, is the command (or hyphen). The shell needs the root password. Click"Enter"after typing the password.

When done whatever you have wanted as root (and you can do something as root), type exit to return to your usual username.

Rather than using the su - command to gain root access, type sudo followed by the command you want to run as root. Since you do not get to set up a root user when you install Ubuntu, you must use the sudo command. Sudo executes the command as if you were logged in as root if you are identified as an authorized user in the /etc/sudoers file. To learn more about the /etc/sudoers file, type man sudoers.

## 5.5 Working with the Date and Time

The date command can show the current date and time and set a new date and time. If you type the date at the shell prompt, you will get something like this: Fri Mar 12 15:10:00 EST 2021

The date command alone, as you can see, shows the latest date and time.

To change the date, log in as root and type date, followed by the date and time in MMDDhhmmYYYY Type March 12, 2021, 10:30 p.m. to set the date and time.

031220302021 is the date.

The date and time format MMDDhhmmYYYY is similar to the 24-hour military clock and has the following meaning:

- MM stands for month and is a two-digit number (01 through 12).

- DD is a two-digit number that represents the month's day (01 through 31).

- In 24-hour format, hh is a two-digit hour (00 is midnight, and 23 is 11 p.m.).

- The minute is measured by mm, which is a two-digit number (00 through 59).

- The four-digit year is denoted by YYYY (such as 2021).

Cal is another useful date-related command. It prints a calendar for the month if you type cal with no choices. When you type cal followed by a number, the number is treated as the year, and the calendar for that year is printed. Provide the month number (1 = January, 2 = February, and so on) accompanied by the year to display the calendar for a particular month in a specific year.

## CHAPTER 6
# BASIC NETWORK ADMINISTRATION

Since most PCs are now connected to a local-area network (LAN) or the Internet, you must also control your network link. To set up the LAN, Linux includes a network configuration tool. A GUI Internet dial-up tool is normally available for connecting to the Internet with a modem.

If you use a DSL or cable modem to link to the Internet, you will need a PC with an Ethernet card that links to the cable or DSL modem. You must also configure the Ethernet card and set up a LAN. Fortunately, these steps are usually included in the Linux installation process. You can use a GUI network configuration tool to do the configurations later if you prefer.

Linux also comes with tools for configuring a firewall, which acts as a security shield between your device and anyone attempting to snoop on your Internet connection. The firewall can be configured using iptables commands or a GUI firewall configuration function.

### Securing Linux on Networking:

A physical channel connects your device to the provider's server, allowing you to connect to the Internet. A physical relation can be arranged in one of three ways:

- A wireless connection;

- A local network;

- A modem that allows PPP to be exchanged.

A wireless access point is required in the first case. It is only possible to set up a wireless network with the Internet if it is open.

When your machine is linked to a local network, the second approach is used to access the World Wide Web via a server. In this scenario, you will not have to worry about setting up the link because the local network administrator will take care of it. Simply open a window, type in the URL you want to visit and go.

The third choice is to use a dial-up modem link. The administrator will not assist you, so you must do it independently. We agreed to investigate this approach further.

You will need a modem and a phone to get started. The next step is to choose an Internet service provider and obtain the phone number from which your PC can connect to the provider's modem pool, and your username and password to enter the global network.

The PPP protocol must then be configured. You can do this manually or help with the configuration software.

Manual configuration is time-consuming and necessitates the editing of files and developing scripts. Beginners should use a particular program that automates the entire process of establishing Internet access.

This software was initially used in the KDE graphical environment and is known as kppp. This utility makes it much easier to set up a link and, usually, you have only to define the accounting details correctly.

<u>Understanding the Internet:</u>

Given the Internet's widespread usage and popularity, you will want to link your Linux device not just to a network but also to the world's largest network: the Internet. Depending on whether you have a DSL or cable modem, I show you how to connect to the Internet in several ways in this chapter. A small percentage of people still use the dial-up network service, but they are few these days. most users are not happy with the slower output of a dial-up connection.

DSL and cable modem are two options for connecting to the Internet, including connecting a particular modem to an Ethernet card on your Linux device. In these situations, you will need to configure your Linux system's Ethernet networking. If your computer is just a client on a network connected to through a mobile/Wi-Fi link and does not need its dedicated connection, things are simple. You will just want to skip through this chapter before moving on to the next.

Your viewpoint on the Internet defines how you interpret it. The majority of people view the Internet through the lens of the services they use. As a user, you might think of the Internet as a medium for exchanging information, with features like:

- **Email:** Use specific email addresses to send emails to everyone on the Internet.

- **Web:** Download and access documents from millions of servers worldwide, link on Facebook, use Google to search for information, and so on.

- **Sharing of information:** Download apps, music files, videos, and other helpful material. You can provide files for users on other systems to download.

- **Remote access:** Log in to another device over the Internet, assuming you have permissions and access to the remote computer.

The Internet, according to technologists, is a global network system. The word internet is an abbreviation for internetworking, which is connecting networks. The Internet Protocol (IP) was developed to link multiple networks.

The Internet equals a network of highways and roads in terms of physical links. Because of this resemblance, the Internet was dubbed "the Information Superhighway" by the mainstream press. The Internet has some very high-capacity networks (a 10-Gbps backbone can support 10 billion bits per second) and many lower-capacity networks ranging from 56 Kbps dial-up connections to a high-speed cable link of 100 Mbps or more, much as the highway and road network has interstate highways, many state roads, and many more suburban streets. (A thousand bits per second equals Kbps, and a million bits per second equals Mbps.)

The Internet's backbone is a high-capacity network.

A single entity does not own the Internet, and it is also not controlled by a single computer. The actual Internet can be viewed as a set of networks operated by thousands of cooperating organizations. Yes, networks are overseen by tens of thousands of companies. It sounds incredible, but it works.

## 6.1 Networking 101

If you are on a computer connected to a LAN and installed the networking during installation, you could already be linked to the Internet.

Allowing Linux to be used for high-speed networks should not be discouraged by high-speed providers. Just because they do not explicitly support Linux does not mean the technology is not compatible with it. TCP/IP (the Internet's collection of traffic rules) was built for the UNIX operating system, from which Linux is descended.

If you want to dual-boot Windows and Linux, your ISP can help you set up your broadband link, and then you can tinker with having Linux connected whenever you have the time and desire.

**Cable modems:** When you sign up for cable Internet service, you will usually be given a particular cable modem system by the installation technician. The signal to the cable modem is carried by either wired coaxial cables or fiber optics. Your workstation can be directly linked to the cable modem through an Ethernet cable connected to an Ethernet port on the cable modem or wirelessly if your workstation has a wireless network chipset. You will need to speak with your cable provider to determine the exact speeds available.

**Digital Subscriber Line (DSL):** DSL sends data in a digital format to your phone jack. DSL is famous because it makes use of your phone company's existing copper telephone wiring. Even the same phone line as a standard phone line can be used. A DSL connection necessitates additional communication hardware, which should be provided by your Internet Service Provider (ISP).

DSL comes in several categories:

> ISDN (Integrated Services Digital Network) Digital Subscriber Line (IDSL) — a description of ISDN can be found later in this bulleted list.

* Optical Subscriber Line (Symmetric) (SDSL)

* Digital Subscriber Line (Asymmetric) (ADSL)

* DSL (Generic) (XDSL)

Ask your ISP about the speed of your DSL link because it varies.

**ISDN (Integrated Services Digital Network):** ISDN is one of the oldest high-speed solutions for homes. When 28 Kbps (half the speed of today's standard dial-up modems) was about all you could get out of the copper strands connecting your phone to the telephone company, it seemed. ISDN is still available in some regions, and it guarantees a constant 128 Kbps connection if you are within 3.4 miles of the phone company's central office.

An ISDN modem (typically supplied by the ISDN ISP) and a network adapter must use ISDN (sometimes an Ethernet card).

**Satellite modems:** For those who live in remote or low-infrastructure areas without access to cable, DSL, or ISDN connections, satellite modems can be a viable option. In several ways, this channel is similar to cable because it is usually accessed from the same providers as satellite television signals. The satellite has certain disadvantages. Your Internet service will suffer the same fate as your satellite television service if it is unreliable. The upload and download speeds can also be very different.

**Dial-up modems:** Even now with high-speed Internet, dial-up modems are still used where broadband is inaccessible or prohibitively costly. It converts the computer's digital signal into the analog signal required for transmission from the phone company's wall jack. You need not do something extra other than subscribing to an ISP since the modem uses an existing voice telephone service. You can't use the same phone line for dial-up and a phone call simultaneously, though.

<u>**Setting up the hardware**</u>:

Before you get too comfortable in your chair, double-check a few items. You will need to perform low-level maneuvers (such as crawling under your desk) to accomplish this:

- **Linking Ethernet cables**: If your cable, DSL, or ISDN modem needs a wired link from your workstation, make sure the following is in place: An Ethernet cable (similar to a phone cable, but with a broader connector) is inserted into your computer's Ethernet port and the particular modem your ISP mounted.

- **Wireless connections:** If your device has a wireless card or chipset, you will need a wireless router to receive and direct your wireless traffic between devices, and a bridge to link your workstation to your Ethernet network. The hardware you are using defines how far and over what (walls, floors, and so on) a wireless router or bridge may be from the card. Setting up your wireless access requires these steps:

- **Identifying the wireless protocol used by your wireless router or bridge:** There are five major types of wireless protocols, which are mostly grouped as Wi-Fi (802.11a, 802.11b, 802.11g, 802.11n, and 802.11ac). Ensure that the wireless router or bridge you buy supports the wireless standard that your devices use.

- Giving your wireless network a unique network name.

- Enabling your wireless network's protection.

There are a few different wireless protection specifications to choose from. The most popular are WEP, WPA, and WPA2, with WPA2 being the most stable of the three. Use WPA2 protection if your wireless router supports it.

**Modem:** If you are using a modem to connect to the Internet, make sure that:

- A telephone cable is inserted into one end of the wall jack and the other end into the modem.

- If using an external modem, make sure the modem is securely linked to the appropriate port on the device and that it is turned on.

- When using an internal modem, double-check that it is not a software modem that requires special Windows drivers (commonly called WinModems).

<u>**Choosing the ISP (Internet Service Provider)**</u>:

Because of Linux's meteoric rise in popularity, many ISPs teach their support staff how to use it. If you already have an ISP, contact them and remind them of your Linux ambitions. Most possibly, the individual already has the information necessary to Linux subscribers and can share it with you. If you are looking for a new Internet service provider, this section will help you make an informed decision.

Some ISPs have proprietary software that must be installed on your computer to connect to the Internet. Likely, the applications they have will only run on Windows.

Consider these questions while looking for an Internet service provider:

- Does it provide Linux technical support? This is an important aspect to remember if you intend to run Linux. It need not be a deal-breaker, but it can be helpful.

- Is it possible to get a recommendation? Inquire with a friend. A happy customer's recommendation is an ISP's best mate.

- Would you be able to use the bandwidth you have agreed to? Many Internet service providers oversubscribe their networks, believing that not all would be online simultaneously. Be getting the bandwidth you are paying for particularly late at night when your neighbors are all watching movies on their computers!

## Gathering The Information You Need:

After you sign up for services with a reliable ISP, you will receive a customer information sheet. This sheet should detail how your network is allocated an IP address needed to communicate over the network. Sometimes, the IP address is allocated to the router, and the individual workstations on your local network are given private IP addresses.

An IP address is allocated to your Linux workstation in one of the two ways:

- **Static:** Your IP address remains the same. Servers use static addresses more often than desktops. Your ISP must provide you with your nameserver IP addresses, gateway address, network address, and netmask if you are using static. The customer information sheet should contain this information.

- **Dynamic:** When you connect, or at regular intervals, your IP address changes. Most desktops do not need the exact address the time, which makes life simpler for ISPs. It also makes life simpler for laptop computers, which are often shifted from network to network. If you are using dynamic addressing, you will be told to use the Dynamic Host Configuration Protocol to bind (DHCP). Your cable, DSL, ISDN, or satellite modem doubles as a router with DHCP, assigning unique IP addresses to devices on your local network.

If you use your ISP as your email provider, you will need to know these additional details to configure your email client.

- The address of the outbound SMTP relay server used to send email messages to the Internet.

- The inbound POP3 or IMAP email server address for retrieving emails from your server's inbox.

You can use your Linux system to create an Internet connection with these details.

## 6.2 Linux Cloud Hosting

Are you looking for Linux Cloud Hosting Servers? To make your website or e-commerce website more effective while still ensuring excellent overall efficiency, this is the better option.

Clients that use Linux Cloud Hosting Servers benefit from improved reconfigurability and the ability to make adjustments based on their qualifications. This hard drive server we provide for you increases your website's overall efficiency and gives you more control over the computing assets available.

Linux server software uses cutting-edge technology to allow anyone to run their version of Linux while also providing them with improved overall performance, tougher reconfigurability, and better supply routes.

One hundred percent uptime is assured, which ensures that your blog can run smoothly without lagging for an extended time. To ensure that your blog is still about backup servers, an auto-failover feature is available.

DDOS Safety is included with the Linux server web hosting service to ensure the highest level of state-of-the-art security. DNS and clientele geographically repetitive are forwarded to eight transit firms.

Linux Shared Web Hosting supports the most recent and dependable web hosting versions, such as Fedora 7, CentOS 7, Ubuntu 14. 04 LTS, and Debian 7. 8. Clients have access to all server and PC functionality of the operating system. These pre-installed hosts are instantly accessible, allowing clients to use them in their own web hosting service offerings.

If you have an issue with your website, there are dedicated support staff available to provide specialized solutions. Any popular and broad understanding foundation can be offered to clients to direct them through simple requests.

Customers are given personal hard drives built to order in the same way as a physical server. The Linux web hosting service program allows your hosts to connect to the Internet via Internap's carrier's gigabit uplinks.

The most recent section variations are provided so the clients can have complete control.

Since the carrier's networks slice up the individual hosts to conveniently share them with the clients, the traditional VPS web hosting service is no longer a preferred option.

VPS providers use container technology to isolate multiple users on a single Linux type, which reduces operation and productivity.

## 6.3 The Network Topology

From Windows to macOS, most modern operating systems have built-in support for Transmission Control Protocol/Internet Protocol (TCP/IP) networking. TCP/IP networking is possible over various physical interfaces, including Ethernet cards, serial ports, and parallel ports.

Usually, an Ethernet network is used for your local area network (LAN) at your office or even at home (if you have two or more systems at home), while wireless (the next chapter) is becoming more common in most areas.

You can use a wireless Ethernet network if you have laptop computers on your local area network (LAN) or do not want to run a tangle of wires to connect a PC to the LAN.

In a typical situation, you have a cable modem or DSL Internet connection. You want to link one or more laptops with wireless network cards to the cable or DSL modem to access the Internet. This chapter explains how to link to an Ethernet LAN and access the Internet using wireless networking.

### 6.3.1 Understanding TCP/IP of LAN

The simplest way to consider TCP/IP networking is to think of it as a four-layer model, with each layer responsible for a specific role. The layered model depicts the data flow between the network's physical link and the end-user application.

| 4 | **Application** | Mail, Transfer, TELNET |
|---|---|---|
| 3 | **Transport** | TCP (Transmission Control Protocol) UDP (User Diagram Protocol) |
| 2 | **Network** | IP (Internet Protocol) |
| 1 | **Physical** | Ethernet |

Information often passes from one layer to the next in this four-layer model. When an application sends data to another application, the data travels across these layers: application, transport, network, and physical. The data is sent up from the physical network transport application to the receiving end.

For handling and formatting data, each layer has its own set of protocols — conventions. A standard protocol is the desired sequence of acts for a mission, such as addressing an envelope, if you think of sending data as being close to sending letters via the postal service (first the name, then the street address, followed by the city, state, and zip or other postal code).

These four layers have different names depending on which reference you check. The transport layer is known as host-to-host. The network layer is known as internetwork or Internet.

The application layer is known as process/application, and the physical layer is known as network access in the old DOD model.

From top to bottom, here's what the four layers do:

- Application: Runs user-facing programs such as email clients, file transfers, and web browsers. Simple Mail Transfer Protocol (SMTP) and Post Office Protocol (POP) for email, Hypertext Transfer Protocol (HTTP) for the Internet, and File Transfer Protocol (FTP) for file transfers are application-level protocols. A port number is often assigned to application-level protocols and can be considered an identifier for a particular application. HTTP or a web server, for example, is connected with port 80.

- Transport: Moves information from one application to another. Transmission Control Protocol (TCP) and User Datagram Protocol (UDP) are the two most relevant protocols in this layer (UDP). TCP ensures data transmission, while UDP simply sends data without ensuring that it reaches its intended destination.

- Network: Receives data packets from one network and transfers them to another. Data packets are routed from one network to the next before they hit their destinations if the networks are far apart. The Internet Protocol is the most important in this layer (IP).

- Physical: The physical networking hardware holds data packets in a network (such as an Ethernet card or token ring card).

The layered model's simplicity is that each layer is responsible for just one mission, leaving the other layers to handle the rest. Layers can be mixed and matched. A TCP/IP network can be built on any form of physical network medium, from Ethernet to radio waves (in a wireless network). Each layer can be implemented in various modules, and the program is modular. The transport and network layers are typically included with the operating system, and any application may use them.

TCP/IP has made substantial strides due to the availability of secure, usable applications. The TCP/IP protocols began as working applications rather than a paper summary of network architecture and protocols — and who can argue with what is already working? TCP/IP now dominates the Internet.

## IP Addresses:

When you have a network with many machines, you need to classify each one individually. The IP address is a computer's address in TCP/IP networking. The address is founded on a network address, and a host address since TCP/IP is concerned with internetworking. You may think of a network address and a host address as having to have two addresses to identify a computer uniquely:

- The network address specifies the computer's location on the network.

- A host address identifies a particular device on a network.

An IP address is a 4-byte (32-bit) value that combines the network and host addresses. Each byte should be written as a decimal value, with a dot (.) after each number. So network addresses like 132.250.112.52 appear. Dotted-decimal or dotted-quad notation is a method of writing IP addresses.

A byte (which has 8 bits) may have a value between 0 and 255 in decimal notation. A valid IP address may contain dotted-decimal numbers only between 0 and 255.

## Port numbers and internet services:

Since several standard services are available on any device that supports TCP/IP, the TCP/IP protocol suite has become the Internet's lingua franca. These services keep the Internet running by making it easier to send and receive email, news, and web pages. These services are recognized by a variety of names, including:

- **DHCP** (Dynamic Host Configuration Protocol) is a protocol that enables a device to configure TCP/IP network parameters dynamically. DHCP is a protocol that assigns dynamic IP addresses and other networking information (such as name servers, default gateways, and domain names) to TCP/IP networks. On port 67, the DHCP server is listening.

- **FTP** (File Transfer Protocol) is a protocol for transferring data over the Internet between computers. FTP uses two ports: port 20 for data transfer and port 21 for control information exchange.

- Domain names are translated into IP addresses using **DNS** (Domain Name System). The port number for this service is 53.

- **HTTP** (Hypertext Transfer Protocol) is a protocol for exchanging documents between computers. The World Wide Web's underlying protocol is HTTP. The web server and client communicate on port 80 by default. As SSL/TLS is added, the protocol becomes HTTPS, and the port number is changed to 443.

- **SMTP** (Simple Mail Transfer Protocol) is a protocol for sending and receiving email messages between systems. For information sharing, SMTP uses port 25.

- The client receives mail using **POP3** (Post Office Protocol version 3), which uses port 110. The port changes to 995 when SSL/TLS is used for protection.

- Clients may also use **IMAP** (Internet Message Access Protocol) to communicate with mail (instead of POP3), and it uses port 143. The port changes to 993 when SSL/TLS is used for security.

• **NNTP** (Network News Transfer Protocol) is a protocol for transmitting news articles around the Internet in a store-and-forward format. The NNTP protocol uses port 119.

• **NetBIOS** is a networking protocol used by Windows, and it uses several ports for the session, the most common of which is 139.

• **SSH** (Protected Shell) is a secure remote login and other secure network services protocol used on an unstable network. Port 22 is used by SSH.

• When a user on one device logs in to another system on the Internet, **Telnet** is used. (To log in to the remote device, the user must have a valid user ID and password.) By default, Telnet connects to port 23, but the Telnet client can link to any port.

• **SNMP** (Simple Network Management Protocol) is a protocol that allows you to manage all forms of network devices over the Internet. SNMP uses the same two ports as FTP: 161 and 162.

• Cisco's Rendezvous Directory Service uses port 465.

• **TFTP** (Trivial File Transfer Protocol) is a file transfer protocol that allows you to pass files from one device to another. (It is usually used to import boot files from another network host through X terminals and diskless workstations.) On port 69, TFTP data is transferred.

• **NFS** (Network File System) is a file-sharing system that allows computers to share files. NFS uses Sun's Remote Procedure Call (RPC) facility, which communicates over port 111.

Each service is connected to a well-known terminal. Each port is used by the TCP protocol to locate a service on any device. (Each service is provided by a server process, a particular computer program that runs on a system.)

## 6.3.2 Understanding Wireless Networks

You have heard of Wi-Fi. Wireless Fidelity (Wi-Fi) is a short-range wireless network that operates similarly to wired Ethernet networks. The technical details of how Wi-Fi networks operate are described by IEEE (Institute of Electrical and Electronics Engineers) standards. Manufacturers use these specifications to develop the products you can purchase to set up a wireless local-area network (WLAN).

The Wi-Fi network norm has progressed quickly. 802.11a gave birth to 802.11b, and the two were merged to form 802.11g, which 802.11n eventually superseded. But the goal of both of these standards was to explain how the physical layer of a wireless Ethernet network functions. You need not know all the specifics of all those specifications to set up a wireless network, but learning a few key points will help you buy the right equipment for your network.

Since all radio channel users share that bandwidth, the actual data throughput that a user sees is still much less than the channel's total capacity. Also, as the distance between the user's PC and the wireless access point grows, the data transfer rate decreases.

## The infrastructure, ad hoc modes, and Wired Equivalent Privacy (WEP):

For wireless Ethernet networks, the 802.11 protocol specifies two modes of operation: ad hoc and infrastructure. Without an access point, ad hoc mode is essentially two or more wireless Ethernet cards communicating with each other.

Infrastructure mode describes how all wireless Ethernet cards communicate with one another and with the wired LAN through an access point. We will assume you have set your wireless Ethernet card to infrastructure mode for this chapter. This mode is called controlled in the configuration files.

Wired Equivalent Privacy (WEP) is a feature of the 802.11 standard that protects wireless communications from eavesdropping. WEP uses a hidden key of 40 or 104 bits exchanged between a mobile station (such as a laptop with a wireless Ethernet card) and an access point (also called a base station). Until data packets are transmitted, the secret key is used to encrypt them, and an integrity check is conducted to ensure that packets are not changed in transit.

The 802.11 standard does not mention how the shared key is created. Many wireless LANs use a single key that all mobile stations and access points exchange. However, in a setting like a college campus, such a method does not scale well because the keys are shared with all users — and you know how it is when you share a password with hundreds of people.

WEP is seldom used on large wireless networks, such as universities. Other authentication approaches, such as SSH (Secure Shell), must log in to remote systems in such wireless networks. Although WEP was once considered adequate for use on a home wireless network, it is no longer recommended.

The Wi-Fi Alliance released a specification called Wi-Fi Protected Access (WPA) more than a decade ago, which replaced the previous WEP standard and enhanced protection by making a few improvements. Unlike WEP, which uses fixed keys, WPA uses Temporal Key Integrity Protocol (TKIP), which creates new keys for every 10 KB of data sent over the network, making WPA more challenging to crack.

Wi-Fi Protected Access 2 (WPA2), the second generation of WPA encryption, was launched by the Wi-Fi Alliance in 2004. WPA2 is based on the final IEEE 802.11i standard, which uses public-key encryption with digital certificates and a RADIUS (Remote Authentication Dial-In User Service) server for authentication, authorization, and accounting in wireless Ethernet networks. WPA2 encrypts data using the Advanced Encryption Standard (AES). WPA3, which was recently revealed, seems to be the way of the future, aiming to raise security even further.

### a.    Main Protocols of the Internet

The Internet Protocol establishes network boundaries and relaying datagrams that allow internet networking.

The structure consists of a header and a payload, the header of which is considered the primary IP address and interfaces linked using specific parameters. Internal and external gateway protocols, and routing prefixes, and network designation, are all concerned. End-to-end protocols play a role in the reliability, but expect the framework to look like this:

UDP Header | UDP DATA → Transport

IP Header | IP Data → Internet

Frame Header | Frame Data | Frame Footer → Link

Data → Application

## Obtaining Information about Peers

To get peer information, return all TCP and IP information. Both the server and the client are linked to the network this way. You may also use the getpeername() socket to capture and save information when it becomes usable quickly. This includes the correct data to be sent and retrieved by different Linux methods and proper socket descriptors and rights for those in the program. Some can also be considered private to improve the user experience.

Allow the socket TCPAcceptor::accept() to be prevalent in the network to accept data. You can say the difference between server and client behavior this way.

## Creating and Destroying

These are linked to the socket's descriptor and allow peer TCP Ports and IP Addresses to be displayed onscreen. Unlike its Linux predecessors, this uses no other languages other than C++.

Destructors could then break any links you have made. To log out of one of your social networking accounts, for example, do so because destructors are present. Most Linux distributions have many programs that can be used for most of your everyday computing needs. Most of these programs can be accessed from your distro's GUI desktop.

Almost every Linux program has a dedicated website where you can find extensive information about it, including where and how to download it. Each distro comes with its collection of utilities and applications you can install when you set up your system.

If a Debian or Debian-based distro, such as Ubuntu, lacks an app, you can quickly get it as long as you have a high-speed internet connection.

## Linux and STMP Client:

SMTP Client is likely to use some of the same characters as before, with a few tweaks. This is all about opening the socket, opening the input and output sources, reading and writing the socket, and cleaning up the client portal. Also, be mindful that it entails:

- Transmission of datagrams. This means that if your portal sends datagrams to different clients and servers, local sockets will operate.

- Linux Communications Stream and datagram communication.

- Socket Programming.

## Echo Client Set-ups

In Linux, Echo Clients operate by passing arguments to the socket (), which means you can use the IP with the PF INET feature to put them both in the same TCP socket. To build a proper client structure, remember that you will need to improve previous codes.

## The Sockets in Linux

Also, be aware that you can code Linux in C because they both use sockets. The socket acts as a bridge between the client and the port and sends the requests to the server while waiting for it to respond. Finally, data transmission and reception are completed.

Simultaneously, the Linux Socket will build a socket for the server, connecting itself to the port. You can listen to client traffic as it builds up. You could also wait for the client to arrive at that stage and watch the data submitted and received. The following are some of its other functions:

| | |
|---|---|
| **socket_description** | This allows both the client and the server's details to appear on screen. |
| **write buffer** | This identifies the information. |
| **write buffer length** | You will need to look at the output of the string to write the buffer length. |
| **client_socket** | The socket definition will appear. |
| **address** | This is used in the link function to keep the address line at the top of the stack. |
| **address_len** | This will appear onscreen if the second parameter is null. |
| **return** | This aids in the return of both the client and the socket outline. Interaction between the client and the server is often simplified because of this. |
| **server_socket** | This is the Description of the top-of-the-head socket. |
| **backlog** | This is the number of demands that have yet to be fulfilled. |

## 6.4 Diagnostic Commands and Files

Setting up Transmission Control Protocol/Internet Protocol (TCP/IP), like almost everything else in Linux, involves preparing a slew of configuration files (text files you can edit with any text editor) and commands. The /etc. The directory contains the majority of these files.

The Linux installer tries to help pre-filling values and remove the need for you to communicate directly with each TCP/IP configuration file. However, if you know the file names and their purposes, manually editing the files (if necessary) is always easier.

When you install Linux, you can set up TCP/IP networking. However, to control the network successfully, you will need to become familiar with the TCP/IP configuration files and be able to edit them if necessary.

(For example, to verify if the name servers are correctly listed, you will need to know about the /etc/resolv.conf file, which stores name server IP addresses.)

| File Name | Contents: |
|---|---|
| /etc/hosts | IP addresses and hostnames for your local network and any other systems you access often |
| /etc/host.conf | Instructions on how to translate hostnames into IP addresses |
| /etc/networks | Names and IP addresses of networks |
| /etc/ nsswitch.conf | Instructions on how to translate hostnames into IP addresses |
| /etc/hosts.allow | Instructions on which systems can access Internet services on your system |
| /etc/resolv.conf | IP addresses of name servers |
| /etc/hosts.deny | Instructions on which systems must be denied access to Internet services on your system |

It is rare to come across a Linux machine not linked to the network, whether it is a computer or a workspace. It is sometimes essential to diagnose network faults, irregular communication, or sluggishness. In this section, we will go through the most widely used Linux commands for network diagnostics.

| COMMAND | PURPOSE |
|---|---|
| ping | It helps in determining the internet connection |
| traceroute | It helps in checking the route jumps needed to connect to the Internet |

| route | Allows to see the route used to connect to the Internet |
|---|---|
| dig | Helps to verify the DNS stability |
| ethtool | Allows to check physical connectivity of network card |
| IP ADDR LS | Lists network cards with their IP addresses<br>Used to configure multiple IP Addresses |
| ifconfig | Shows the network configuration of the network cards |
| mtr | Used to determine the routers having delays in network response and traffic |
| nslookup | Used to check the IP address of the desired host/websi |

CHAPTER 7

# ALTERNATIVES TO WINDOWS APPLICATIONS

"What application is available on Linux?" and "Would I be enabled to utilize my preferred applications and programs on Linux? These are two of the most commonly asked questions about Linux.

While the same program might be readily accessible on Linux sometimes, it is not in the majority of the cases. The best part is that Linux has a multitude of substitutes to the most common Windows programs.

This chapter will teach you about some of the finest applications for Linux. We will look at Microsoft Office, Photoshop, Internet Explorer, Windows Media Player, Adobe Reader, and other software alternatives.

## 7.1 Microsoft Office Substitute

Productivity is an essential feature of every operating system or platform. Fortunately, Linux has a wide range of productivity applications, including office suites.

The majority of MS Office substitutes for Linux may download and be used to access, modify, and generate documents in many file types, including .xlsx, .docx, and .pptx.

**LibreOffice:** On Linux, LibreOffice is commonly regarded as the best Microsoft Office substitute. Many Linux computers and distros come with it as the standard office suite. It is partly because it is free and open-source. This is because it is amazing.

It is not Microsoft Office, but it is a substitute, and becoming used to Libre Office will be difficult at first if you are used to Microsoft's offering.

As you get used to it and become more familiar with it, you will discover that Libre Office is just as feature-rich, if not more so. LibreOffice is a fork of OpenOffice, which was widely used before LibreOffice. Since it is open-source software, it has access to a large developer community. Essentially, everyone can help with the venture. LibreOffice supports plug-ins to make it simpler for sure developers.

If there is anything you think is missing, look around to see if you can find an extension that incorporates the feature/function you are looking for. It is compatible with all three big desktop operating systems, and Linux.

Advantages:

- It is open-source and free.

- Full functionality is provided.

- Compatibility with Microsoft Office file types is excellent.

Downsides:

- The style is obsolete.

**Apache OpenOffice:** OpenOffice is based on the same framework as LibreOffice and also has a lot in common with it.   Due to the long development cycle, it lags behind LibreOffice in terms of development. One of the critical reasons LibreOffice broke away from them was because of this.

Apache OpenOffice is a reasonable MS Office replacement for Linux. Years of development and testing have gone into it, and it, like LibreOffice, is cross-platform. It has a lot of features for making papers, presentations, and sheets. This substitute office suite incorporates Microsoft Office formats besides the traditional open document format.

This ensures that the documents you distribute or obtain from Microsoft Office users are compatible.

Advantages:

- A familiar and straightforward user interface.

- The Apache license is used.

- Many languages are supported.

Negative aspects:

- Microsoft Office file formats have little support.

## 7.2 MS Notepad Substitute

Notepad is a standard source code and text editor among programmers and the public but it is only compatible with Windows. On Linux, however, there is a range of competent or even superior alternatives.

**Vim:** Vim is, without question, one of the most helpful word processors for programming in Linux. Since its emergence as Vi, it has gained widespread popularity and has developed itself as among the most influential editors in the Unix world. Consider Vim highly recommended if you are searching for a compact, revolutionary, and configurable Notepad alternative for Linux. Multi-level undo chains, comprehensive support for various plug-ins and file types, and fully prepared compatibility with many tools are just a few of Vim's notable features.

Some Notable features of Vim:

- Vim's multi-level undo framework is unique in how it gives you complete control over your source code while also allowing you to experiment.

- It provides scripting features and comprehensive support for a handful of computer languages and file formats.

- Vim is exceptionally secure, and it can quickly meet the needs of even the most demanding users.

- It, along with Emacs, is among the most versatile text editors, allowing for a wide range of changes with minimal effort.

**<u>Gedit:</u>** Gedit, like Notepad++, is a small but powerful code editor that runs on Linux, Microsoft Windows, Mac OS, and BSD. External scripting, resources, and snippet compilation, among other features, are all supported extensively. Gedit comes with support for FTP, SSH, HTTP, and WebDAV, among other secure data editing protocols. If you are running Ubuntu or another GNOME-based operating system, Gedit is probably already installed.

Salient Features:

- Gedit is highly customizable, with scripting languages such as HTML, C, C++, Python, XML, and Perl provided.

- Compared to other Notepad alternatives, the find and replace feature is excellent, and regular expressions are supported.

- Gedit has a plug-in framework that lets users add additional features for a much more interactive performance.

- It was first published over two decades ago, but it is still constantly operated and maintained.

## 7.3 Internet Explorer/Microsoft Edge Substitute

Though Internet Explorer has traditionally been the standard web browser for Windows, Linux users have access to various complementary and particularly unique browsers. There's undoubtedly an alternate browser to choose from for you if you are tired of using Microsoft Edge and need a browser to complete a specific project.

**<u>Brave:</u>** Brave reached the browser business in 2016. Brave is browser-centered on the accessible Chromium browser and has great ad and tracking service blocking capabilities. Brave became one of the increasingly commonly preferred browsers in 2019, thanks to its unique privacy features.

Brave recently launched the Basic Attention Token (BAT), a cryptocurrency used to compensate users for displaying ads distributed via Brave's privacy-focused advertisement network. Users can also use BAT to "tip" sites, have Brave distribute BAT to the pages they visit randomly or hold the BAT for trading them in for cash.

Although the company's attempt to disrupt online ads fails in the long term, it is encouraging to see more open source innovation and applications that support Linux. On brave.com, you will find installation instructions.

**Google Chrome:** Google Chrome and its open-source companion Chromium have rapidly become the most common replacements for Microsoft Edge on Ubuntu machines since their release in late 2008. Chromium is available in the Ubuntu packages and can be installed using apt or snap. Chrome is also available directly from Google. Canonical has considered making Chromium the standard browser in Ubuntu in place of Internet Explorer, but Firefox has so far kept its ground.

## 7.4 Photoshop Substitute

Adobe Photoshop is a high-end image development and design program that runs on both Windows and Mac OS X. It is undeniable that almost everyone knows it. It is that well-liked. You can also use Photoshop with Linux in a virtual machine running Windows, but this is not the best experience.

As a general rule, we do not have many choices for Adobe Photoshop replacements. However, we will go through some of the finest free Photoshop substitutes for Linux in this chapter.

**Pixlr:** Pixlr is a free but closed-source online image editing program that allows users to manipulate images creatively using various advanced features and tens of thousands of free effects.

Pixlr's software clients are compatible with Android, Mac os, Windows, and Ios, and it has around 500 million active users more than 10 billion retouched images. Although it does not yet have a Linux app, Linux users can take advantage of all of its capabilities through accessing its online versions to generate and edit beautiful images in their browser.

**Photopea:** Photopea is another free online editing software that allows you to create and manipulate raster images. It operates in the browser and therefore stores data locally, allowing you to use it even though you are not connected to the internet.

Photopea is programmed to emulate Photoshop's user interface and many functions, such as interacting with masks, filters, textures, shapes, intelligent artifacts, and key bindings. Other standard graphical formats like RAW, PSD, sketch, and XCF are also supported.

You can not go mistaken with Photopea if you would like a legitimately free editing software you can run on any device. It is freely available to access if you do not like the advertisements shown.

## 7.5 Movie Maker Substitute

Windows Movie Maker was one of the main reasons Video Production & Video Editing became regarded as a simple task, as the software allowed developers to blend multiple videos with various effects and everything. Its interface was so simple that almost any user could grasp the mechanism in a matter of seconds. However, it is understandable if you deem Movie Maker lacking in certain areas, including when you require extra functionality or would like to edit videos on a system for which Movie Maker is not accessible.

However, for video processing, you could need a more sophisticated environment. Here are a few windows movie maker alternatives you can choose while using Linux:

### Shotcut

Shotcut is a video editing app for Linux, and it is peculiar in that its user interface resembles that of a media player rather than an editor. With its extensive collection of features, the app makes video editing a breeze. It will suffice for most purposes, but if you require more robust features, such as specialized or advanced video recording, this may not be the suitable alternative. It counts as a good video editing software for Linux due to its features.

## Pitivi

Pitivi is a video editor also open-source and free to use. This app is made for simple video editing. Simple functions such as clipping, splitting, trimming, and clip snapping are provided.

Audio mixing is assisted by the Pitivi curves method. It also has the potential to use hotkeys and keyboard shortcuts.

This allows audio and video to be connected, which is a significant gain. It is the only open-source video editor to facilitate the MEF (Material Exchange Format) format.

The user-friendly GUI of Pritivi allows for direct manipulation, drag-and-drop, and native theme navigation.          This program can be converted into several languages. It also comes with a user manual.

## 7.6 Windows Media Center Substitute

Here are a few alternatives to the Windows Media Center which you can use on Linux:

## GeeXboX

GeeXboX is a full-featured Linux media center operating system that runs on laptops and embedded computers. It can be run directly from a USB stick or built conventionally, and it has a small footprint.

The most recent edition, 3.1, is just 160 megabytes in size. GeeXboX is ideal for running on older machines or booting from a USB drive. Since GeeXboX is built on Kodi, you will recognize the user interface.

### OpenELEC

OpenELEC ran XBMC, but it has since evolved to run Kodi. Installing the destination folder on a spare hard disc partition is all that is needed. Your Linux machine will run Kodi once it is done.

With connections to the entire Kodi add-on collection, you can customize your Linux media center to your liking.

Kodi also supports live Television and DVR, offering you a complete media center environment.

## 7.7 Adobe Acrobat Reader Substitute

Adobe Reader has long been regarded as one of the best PDF readers and editors on most Desktop systems. The free edition of Adobe Reader contains features such as document reading and viewing, printing, and annotations. The PRO edition, a premium version, adds features including PDF editing, transformation, and signing.

Other PDF readers offer identical core functions for daily use. There are many PDF reader applications to choose from, based on the number of features needed. Some focus on providing basic functionality, whereas others provide extra features to enhance functionality.

### X-PDF

It performs the essential tasks that a reader would anticipate. The text extraction process, PDF to Postscript conversion, and other utilities are among the functions. Consumers who prefer graphical user interfaces can be confused. It is available for download through the download page or the Linux terminal.

### GNU GV

It is a simple graphical user interface (GUI) framework for displaying PDF documents on Linux.

It operates by allowing users to communicate primarily with Ghost script parser via a user interface.

It also has an outdated user interface that does not appeal to those who require brightly colored graphics. It is, however, compact and practical for basic PDF tasks like viewing, printing, and zooming. You can use the apt package manager, dnf for Fedora, or yum for CentOS to install it on Ubuntu-based distros.

# CONCLUSION

This book has helped you learn how to use Linux with confidence, from installing it on your computer to writing your programs.

We also hope this book has helped you select the best Linux distribution for your needs and applications to assist you in performing everyday computing tasks. You should also have learned how to work inside a Linux environment using the command line by the end of this book, and some steps for making your system stable.

Linux is unquestionably one of the most dependable Operating Systems available—and the best part is that it is free, so you will not have to pay extra to get it, and you will not have to settle for counterfeit copies because you cannot afford the legal edition.

Working with Linux does not require years of hands-on experience, loads of trial and error, advanced computer science training, or deep commitment, as it appears at first glance. You can create a Linux system that does what you want if you can tell anyone how to find your office.

The aim of this book is not to transform you into a full-fledged Linux geek (although that is the pinnacle of Linux enlightenment). Instead, it is to show you the ins and outs of building a well-functioning Linux system and to give you the know-how and ability to use it.

That is all you will need to get started with Linux. You will need a text editor, the Linux shell, or an integrated development environment, and knowledge of a programming language besides a decent, reliable computer and a Linux distribution to be a Linux professional.

Now is the time to put your skills to the test and analyze what you have learned so far from this book.

I thank you personally for your investment and your time, please don't forget to leave a review on the platform where you found this guide, it helps me to know better my readers and enrich my next publications.

Thank you again in advance.

**Hey! And don't miss these ones! I'm sure that you will be interested:**

## DELVE INTO THE WORLD OF CRYPTOCURRENCY AND BLOCKCHAIN WITH THIS COMPREHENSIVE GUIDE!

Blockchain and Cryptocurrency are a part of the global phenomenon that has taken over the world. They are a modern wave of innovation that is already reshaping the industry, social and political relationships, and every other form of exchanging value.

Still, they seem so alien, and it seems like nobody knows anything about them. Mainstream media is riddled with mysteries, myths, and partial answers to many questions regarding crypto.

What exactly are cryptocurrencies?

How does blockchain technology work?

How are they related to real-world currencies such as the US dollar or the Euro?

How can they be obtained?

This book bridges the gap between strictly technical books about the blockchain and research-based books primarily concerned with practical applications, discussions of its expected economic effect, and future visions.

It will be your guide through the unknown and complicated world of cryptocurrency and blockchain technology.

## DISCOVER HOW YOU CAN INVEST AND MAKE MONEY WITH CRYPTOS TODAY!

Investing in Cryptocurrencies is an important skill today, there is a lot of information and courses on the internet but learning online can lead to non-useful information and above all to misunderstandings and over-information that will only waste time.
This book will allow you to learn step by step and effectively everything you need to know to invest and earn with crypto.

Would you like to know how you can start investing in cryptos? **If so, then you are in the right place.**

This book is a step-by-step guide that will teach you in an easy and comprehensive way, how you start investing in Cryptocurrencies.

I want to show you some of the things that we are going to cover together in the book so that you can better understand what we are going to learn.

## DISCOVER AND LEARN THE BEST METAVERSE INVESTING STRATEGIES FOR TODAY!

The world of the metaverse is a world in constant growth, a fascinating world full of investment opportunities.
There are many people who try to invest and create profit with this technology but only a few are willing to study and really understand what the metaverse is, how it works, and how the world will develop and change in the coming years.
This is a book that will definitely guide you to learn everything related to the metaverse, with a particular focus on investments in the best digital assets, is an opportunity that you must not miss.

Would you like to learn the best Metaverse Investments? **If so, then you are in the right place.**

I want to show you some of the things that we are going to cover together in the book so that you can better understand what we are going to learn.

**Here are just some of the topics we will touch on together:**

- The True Meaning of Metaverse
- Why the Metaverse is important
- Making Money with NFT's
- Marketing in the Metaverse
- Much more

**If you want to learn the best Metaverse Investment strategies, all you have to do is follow the advice found in this book. So what are you waiting for?**